INTERNATIONAL
Children's
Bible
Dictionary

LYNN WALLER

Consulting Editors: Dr. R. K. Harrison
Dr. Neale Pryor
Educational Editor: Alice Huffaker

WORD PUBLISHING
Dallas·London·Vancouver·Melbourne

INTERNATIONAL
Children's
Bible
Dictionary

Cover Design: Koechel/Peterson Design

Illustrations: David Smith, Smith Design

Library of Congress Number 89-51461
ISBN 0-8499-4013-3 (formerly ISBN 0-8499-0812-4)

Printed in the United States of America
    50 RRD 987

7 8 9 0 1 2 3 4 RRD 9 8 7 6 5 4 3 2 1

How to Use Your Bible Dictionary

What Is a Bible Dictionary?

A dictionary tells you what words mean—their "definitions." A *Bible* dictionary explains what the words found in the Bible mean. It also helps you learn how to say those words. Sometimes it even shows you a picture to help you understand. This dictionary will also tell you some places in the Bible where you can find the word. And it often tells you to look up other words in the dictionary that will help explain even more about the first word you looked up. The *International Children's Bible Dictionary* helps you understand the Bible better!

How to Look up Bible Words
Alphabetical Order: From A-Z

There are thousands of words in the Bible. So, to help you find the exact word you want to know more about, the words in this dictionary follow the order of the alphabet. All the words that start with the letter "a," such as "Adam" and "ark," come first. All the words that start with "b" come next. And on it goes through the whole alphabet until it ends with "z" at the back of the book. Each new word is in heavy black letters so it can be found easily.

Guidewords

Guidewords help you find the right page quickly. You will find guidewords in bold black letters above the line at the top of each page. They are the "start" and "stop" words. The guideword at the top of the left page is the first word on that page. The guideword at the top of the right page is the last word on *that* page. So, all the words on those two pages come between the "start" and "stop" words in alphabetical order. For instance, the start word might be "camel" and the stop word might be "cross." Some of the words on those two pages would be "Cana," "cherubim" and "creation."

How to Say the Word

After each word that is hard to say, you will see the word spelled as it *sounds*. And the part of the word that is to be stressed when you say it is in all capital letters. For instance, the word "Adonijah" is followed by (ad-oh-NY-jah). Some words like "Luke" and "Mark" are easy, and you won't need help to say them.

Where to Find the Word in the Bible

One very special help this Bible dictionary gives you is where to find each word in the Bible. At the end of the word definition will be a list of some places in the Bible where that word appears. It will give you the name of the Bible book, the chapter and the verse. "Goliath," for instance, can be found in 1 Samuel 17:4 (the first book of Samuel, chapter 17, verse 4).

How to Learn More about a Word

This Bible dictionary helps you learn even more about some words than just their meanings. Some words have pictures to help you understand them better, like "adder" and "rock badger." And some words tell you to "See" (look up) another word in the dictionary for more information. For instance, at the end of the definition of "Jesus," it says "See also *Christ* and *Messiah*." You can also learn more about a word by reading the verses in the Bible where the word appears.

Word Clues

The *International Children's Bible Dictionary* gives you some special word clues to help you understand the language of the Bible more easily. For instance, in the Hebrew language the word "beth" means "house." "Beth" often appears in the Bible connected to another word, such as "Beth-Aven." So, Beth-Aven means "house of Aven." What do you think "Beth-Shemesh" means? Clues are also given about some of our words and phrases today that came from the Bible, such as "apple of my eye," and "handwriting on the wall."

A Message to Parents and Teachers

The *International Children's Bible Dictionary* is an attractive, all-new Bible dictionary written especially for children. While being theologically accurate, it is at the same time simple enough for elementary-aged children to read and understand for themselves. The definitions explain the meanings clearly in a child's terms. These are combined with over 100 realistic illustrations to help the child visualize the idea being defined. "Word Clues" are found throughout to extend the child's learning to other Bible words.

Care has been taken in the *International Children's Bible Dictionary* to include cross-references to such accepted versions of the Bible as the *King James Version* and the *New International Version*, as well as the *International Children's Bible*. In this way the book will be valuable in all Bible study settings—personal study, family devotions, Bible classroom use, Christian school classrooms, church and school libraries and many others.

You will find the *International Children's Bible Dictionary* an excellent addition to a child's library and to his personal understanding of the Bible.

Aaron (AIR-ohn) was the older brother of Moses. He often spoke for Moses. Only men from Aaron's family could be priests. (Exodus 4–40; Numbers 1–25)

Abba (AB-uh) was a child's word for "father" in the Aramaic language. Early Christians used this word in speaking to God. This shows how close we can feel to him. (Mark 14:36; Romans 8:15; Galatians 4:6)

Abednego (a-BED-nee-go) means "servant of Nego." Nego was probably the Babylonian god Nabu. Abednego was one of the three friends of Daniel whom God protected from the fiery furnace. (Daniel 3)

Abel (AY-bul) means "breath." He was the second son of Adam and Eve. He was the first person to be murdered. Cain (his brother) killed him because Cain was jealous. God had been pleased with Abel's sacrifice but not Cain's. (Genesis 4:1-11; Matthew 23:35; 1 John 3:12)

Abib (ah-BEEB) means "young ears of grain." It is the first month of the Jewish calendar and about the time of year as our March or April. It is also called Nisan. (Exodus 13:4; 34:18; Deuteronomy 16:1)

Abigail (AB-eh-gale) means "father of joy." She was the wife of Nabal. After he died she married David. (1 Samuel 25) David also had a sister named Abigail. (1 Chronicles 2:17)

Abijah (a-BY-jah), or Abijam, means "the Lord is my father." It was the name of nine different people in the Old Testament. Some of them are as follows:

Abijah was the name of Jeroboam's son. He was the only one in his family who pleased God. (1 Kings 14:1-18)

Abijah, the king of Judah, was Solomon's grandson. He led his army against Jeroboam and the kingdom of Israel. (1 Kings 15:1-8; 2 Chronicles 12:16–14:1)

Abijah, the son of Samuel, was a dishonest judge. (1 Samuel 8:1-3)

Abib

Abimelech (a-BIM-eh-lek) means "my father is king." It may have been the name given to Philistine kings.

Abimelech, king of Gerar, tried to marry Abraham's wife, Sarah, but God stopped him. (Genesis 20)

Abimelech, a later king of Gerar, thought Isaac's wife, Rebekah, was Isaac's sister. (Genesis 26:6-11)

Abimelech, the son of Gideon, was the king of Shechem. (Judges 8:31−9:57)

Abishai (a-BISH-eye) means "father of a gift." He was a nephew of King David. He served in David's army and was very loyal to him. Once he even saved David from being killed by a giant. (2 Samuel 20:6-7; 21:15-17; 23:18-19; 1 Chronicles 18:12)

Abner (AB-nur) means "father of light." He was the commander of Saul's army. He was also Saul's cousin. When Saul died, Abner tried to make Saul's son Ish-Bosheth the next king. But later he decided that David should be king. (2 Samuel 2−3)

Abraham (AY-brah-ham) was the most respected man in the Jewish nation. The Jews called him "father Abraham." He was known for his great faith. (Genesis 12−25; John 8:39; Romans 4:1,16; Hebrews 11: 11-12)

Absalom (AB-sah-lum) means "father of peace." He was one of David's sons. He tried to take over David's kingdom. But he was killed when his hair got caught in a tree as he tried to escape on horseback. (2 Samuel 13−18)

abyss (uh-BISS) See "bottomless pit."

Achaia (a-KA-yuh) See "Greece."

Achan (AY-can) means "troublesome." He was an Israelite who disobeyed God during the battle of Jericho. He secretly stole some valuables from Jericho. God caused Israel to lose its next battle because of this sin. (Joshua 7:1-26)

Achish (AY-kish) was king of the Philistine city of Gath. He allowed David to stay in his city for awhile when Saul was chasing David. (1 Samuel 21:10-15; 29:1-11; 1 Kings 2:39-40)

Acts (AX) is the fifth book in the New Testament. It tells how the first followers of Jesus spread the Good News to all parts of the world. It was written by Luke, a doctor who traveled with Paul. Acts especially shows how Peter and Paul led people to become Christians. See "Good News."

Adam (AD-um) means "out of the earth." He was the first man God created. He was made from the dust of the ground. (Genesis 1−4; 1 Corinthians 15:45)

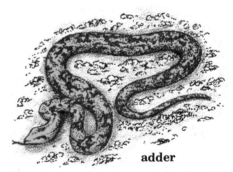

adder

adder is a poisonous snake. In Bible times it was called a "puff adder." See "snake."

Adonijah (ad-oh-NY-jah) means "my lord is the Lord." He was David's fourth son. He tried to make himself king when his father was old. But David stopped him by having Solomon made king. (1 Kings 1-2)

Adoni-Zedek (a-DOH-ny-ZEE-dek) means "lord of justice." He was an Amorite king of Jerusalem. He and four other Amorite kings were defeated by Joshua's army at Gibeon. God helped the Israelites win by making the sun and moon stand still. (Joshua 10:1-28)

Adullam (a-DOO-lum) was a very old city about 13 miles from Bethlehem. David hid in a cave near there when Saul was chasing him. This was when some of David's men risked their lives to get him water from Bethlehem. Read the story to see how David showed his appreciation in an unusual way. (2 Samuel 23:13-17)

adultery (ah-DUL-ter-ee) is breaking a marriage promise by having sexual relations with someone other than your husband or wife. (Exodus 20:14; Mark 10:11-12; John 8:3-5)

Agabus (AG-uh-bus) was a Christian prophet. Twice he told the apostle Paul about something that was going to happen in the future. He said there would be no food in the land. (Acts 11:27-30; 21:10-11)

Agag (AY-gag) was a king of the Amalekites. Saul kept him alive when he was supposed to have killed him. This was one reason God rejected Saul as king. (1 Samuel 15)

agreement (uh-GREE-ment) is a contract or promise. It is sometimes called a covenant. God made agreements with his people. One agreement was the "law of Moses." God has given a new agreement to his people through Christ in the New Testament. Hebrews 8-10 explains the differences between the two agreements. (Genesis 9:9-17; Hebrews 9:15-22)

Agrippa (uh-GRIP-pah) See "Herod Agrippa II."

Ahab (AY-hab) means "father's brother." He was a very evil king of Israel. He was married to Jezebel, who worshiped the false god Baal. This led many of the Israelites away from God. The prophet Elijah tried to show Ahab who the true God was. But Ahab would not listen. So God allowed Ahab to be killed in battle. (1 Kings 16:29-34; 18; 21-22)

Ahasuerus (ah-HAZ-oo-EE-rus) was the name of two men:

    Ahasuerus was the name of the father of Darius the Mede. (Daniel 9:1)

    Ahasuerus, King of Persia, married Esther, a young Jewish woman.

He is known as Xerxes (ZERK-sees) in the history outside of the Bible. (Esther)

Ahaz means "possessor." He was the twelfth king of Judah. He worshiped false gods and even sacrificed his own son to them. (2 Kings 16; 2 Chronicles 28; Isaiah 7)

Ahaziah (ay-ha-ZY-uh) means "held by the Lord." This was the name of two men in the Bible:

Ahaziah, king of Judah, was a nephew of the first Ahaziah. He was murdered by Jehu. (2 Chronicles 22:1-9)

Ahaziah, the son of Ahab, was king of Israel for one year. (1 Kings 22: 40-53; 2 Kings 1)

Ahijah (a-HY-jah) means "brother of the Lord." This was the name of several people in the Bible.

Ahijah, the great-grandson of Eli, was a priest when Saul was king. Once Ahijah brought the ephod (or Holy Vest) of God to the place where Israel was fighting the Philistines. (1 Samuel 14:1-23)

Ahijah, the prophet, lived when Jeroboam was king. Twice he told what would happen to Jeroboam in the future. (1 Kings 11:29-39; 14:1-20)

Ahimelech (a-HIM-eh-lek) means "my brother is the king." He was high priest when Saul was king. When Saul was chasing David, Ahimelech helped David by giving him bread to eat and Goliath's sword to defend himself. (1 Samuel 21–22)

Ahithophel (a-HITH-oh-fel) means "brother of foolishness." He was one of the people who gave David advice when he was king. But when Absalom rebelled against David, Ahithophel joined Absalom's side. Then when Absalom did not listen to his advice, Ahithophel killed himself. (2 Samuel 15:12,31; 16:15–17:23)

Ai (AY-eye) means "the ruin." It was the name of a city the Israelites attacked right after defeating Jericho. Israel lost the first battle because of Achan's sin. The next time Joshua used a trick on the army of Ai. The Israelites completely destroyed the city. It was still in ruins when the book of Joshua was written. But it was rebuilt and is mentioned in later books of the Bible. (Joshua 7–8; Ezra 2:28; Nehemiah 7:32)

Akeldama (a-KEL-dah-mah) means "field of blood." It was the name of the field that was bought with the money Judas received for betraying Jesus. The field was used as a place to bury strangers who died in Jerusalem. (Matthew 27:3-10; Acts 1:18-19)

alabaster (AL-a-bas-ter) is a light-colored stone with streaks or stripes through it. Perfume was often kept in beautiful containers made of alabaster. (Matthew 26:7; Luke 7:37)

alamoth (AL-a-moth) was probably a musical word. It may mean "like a flute" or "high-pitched." (Psalm 46)

All-Powerful (or Almighty) is a name for God in the Bible. The Hebrew word is "El Shaddai." God first used this name to tell Abraham that he would do something that seemed impossible. (Genesis 17:1; Exodus 6:3; Psalm 91:1; Revelation 4:8)

Almighty See "All-Powerful."

almond (AH-mond)·is a common tree in Bible lands. It produces nuts that are good to eat. It is the first tree to blossom each year. Aaron's stick that blossomed was an almond branch. The cups of the golden lampstand in the Holy Tent were shaped

almond

like almond flowers. (Exodus 25:33-36; Numbers 17:8; Jeremiah 1:11)

aloes (AL-ohs) were oils from sweet-smelling sap of certain trees. They were used to make perfume and medicine and to prepare bodies for burial. (Numbers 24:6; John 19:39)

Alpha and Omega (AL-fah and oh-MAY-guh) Alpha is the first letter of the Greek alphabet, like "A" in English. Omega is the last letter of the Greek alphabet, like "Z" in English. Jesus is called the Alpha and the Omega in the Bible. It is a way of saying that he was at the beginning of all things and he will be at the end of all things. (Revelation 1:8; 21:6; 22:13)

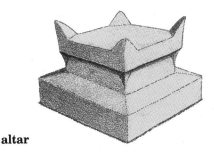

altar

altar (ALL-ter) was a place where sacrifices, gifts or prayers were offered to God. Altars were often made of dirt, grass or rocks piled up in the shape of a table on which the gift could be placed. (Genesis 8:20; 22:9; 1 Kings 18:30-35; Matthew 5:23-24; James 2:21)

Amalekites (AM-a-lah-kites) were fierce, fighting people. These descendants of Esau moved often. For hundreds of years they were enemies of Israel. Moses, Saul and David all led Israel in battle against the Amalekites. They were finally wiped out during the time of Hezekiah. (Genesis 36:12; Exodus 17:8-16; 1 Samuel 15,30; 1 Chronicles 4:43)

Amasa (AM-a-sa) was the leader of Absalom's army when he rebelled against David. After Absalom was killed, David made Amasa the commander of his army. But Joab, who had been David's commander, was angry and killed Amasa. (2 Samuel 17:25; 19:13; 20:1-10)

Amaziah (am-ah-ZY-uh) means "whom the Lord gives strength." He was the ninth king of Judah. He began as a good king. But he became too proud after defeating Edom in battle. He foolishly challenged Israel to fight and lost. Amaziah also started worshiping false gods. Finally, his own people had him killed. (2 Kings 14; 2 Chronicles 25)

amen (AY-MEN or AH-MEN) is a Hebrew word for "that is right." A person says "amen" to show he agrees with what has been said. (1 Chronicles 16:36; Nehemiah 5:13; 8:6; Psalm 106:48; 1 Corinthians 14:16; Revelation 7:11-12)

A

Ammonites (AM-on-ites) were the descendants of Lot's son, Ben-ammi. They lived north of the Dead Sea. Ammonites protected their land by building stone watchtowers. They worshiped the false god Molech and often attacked the Israelites. (1 Samuel 11; 2 Samuel 10; Nehemiah 2:10,19)

Amon (AM-on) means "faithful." He was the fifteenth king of Judah. He ruled for only two years. His son was the good king Josiah. (2 Kings 21: 18-26; 2 Chronicles 33:20-25)

Amorites (AM-or-ites) were a group of people who lived in Canaan when the Israelites arrived. They were a wicked people who worshiped false gods. They were defeated by Joshua and his army. (Genesis 15: 15-16; Joshua 10:1–11:14; Psalm 135: 10-12)

Amos (AY-mos) means "burden bearer." He was a man who took care of sheep and sycamore trees. But God called him to be a prophet. He told the people of Israel they were sinning just like other nations who didn't know God. He warned them that God would punish them if they did not obey him. The Bible book of Amos tells what Amos said. (Amos 1-9)

Anak/Anakites (A-nak/AN-uh-kites) The Anakites were named for their ancestor Anak. They were a group of people who lived in Canaan when the Israelites arrived. They were known as large, mean, fighting people. (Numbers 13:22,28,33; Deuteronomy 1:28; 2:10-11; 9:2; Joshua 11:21-22)

Ananias (an-uh-NY-us) was the name of three different men in the New Testament.

Ananias was punished by death for lying to the Holy Spirit, along with his wife, Sapphira. (Acts 5: 1-6)

Ananias was a Christian in the city of Damascus. God sent him to help Saul of Tarsus when Saul was made blind. (Acts 9:10-19; 22:12-16)

Ananias, the high priest, was at the apostle Paul's trial. (Acts 23: 1-5)

Andrew (AN-droo) was a fisherman and the brother of the apostle Peter. Andrew was also 1 of the 12 apostles of Jesus. (Mark 1:16-18; 3:14-19; John 1:40-44; Acts 1:13)

angel (AIN-jel) is a Greek word that means "messenger." Angels are heavenly beings. They can sometimes look like people. God used angels to help his people and to announce important events. (Genesis 21:17; 22:11-15; Matthew 25:41; Luke 2: 8-15; Hebrews 1:14; 12:22; 13:2; 2 Peter 2:4)

Annas (AN-us) was a high priest of the Jews during Jesus' lifetime. He served as the high priest in Jerusalem from A.D. 7 to 14. (Luke 3:2; John 18:12-23; Acts 4:6) See also "priest."

anoint (uh-NOINT) means to pour oil on a person. Often the oil was used as perfume or just to celebrate a special occasion. Sometimes it was a medicine. People were also anointed to show that they had been appointed to be a prophet, priest or king. (1 Samuel 16:12-13; Psalm 89:20; Mark 6:13; Luke 7:38)

anoint

Antioch (AN-tee-ahk) was a city named for Antiochus, father of Alexander the Great. It was the third largest city in the Roman Empire. Here the followers of Christ were first called by the name "Christians." From this city Paul began his three missionary journeys. Also, the first church of non-Jewish Christians was in Antioch of Syria. Today this city is called Antakya, Turkey. (Acts 11:20-26; 13:1-3)

There was another smaller city named Antioch about 300 miles away in the country of Pisidia. Paul and Barnabas preached there on their first missionary journey. (Acts 13:14-15)

apostle (uh-POS-'l) is a Greek word that means "someone who is sent off." Jesus gave the name to the 12 men he chose as his special followers. He sent them to tell the Good News about him to the whole world. Later, after Judas killed himself, Matthias became an apostle. Paul was also called an apostle. (Matthew 10:1-4; Mark 3:14-19; Acts 1:2-26; 1 Corinthians 15:8-10)

A

Word Clues

apple of his eye
refers to someone who is very special to us. We may say, "He is the apple of my eye." It comes from Moses' song in Deuteronomy 32:10 where he describes how God took care of his people.

Aquila (AK-wi-lah) was a Jewish Christian from the city of Rome. He and his wife Priscilla (or Prisca) worked as tentmakers and traveled with Paul. When they were at home in Rome or working in Ephesus, the Christians worshiped in their home. (Acts 18:2-3,18,26; Romans 16:3-5; 1 Corinthians 16:19)

Arabah (AIR-uh-bah) is the Hebrew word for the Jordan Valley. This includes the lowland from Lake Galilee to the Red Sea. (Deuteronomy 1:1; 3:17; Joshua 11:2)

Arabah, Sea of, See "Dead Sea."

Aram (AIR-um) was a country northeast of Israel. Damascus was its capital. Aram was often at war with Israel and Judah. It is also called Syria. Syria is the name used in the New Testament, and even to today. (Genesis 10:22; 2 Kings 5; Isaiah 7:1-4) See "Syria."

Aramaic (AIR-uh-MAY-ik) was the language of the people in the nation of Aram. The Jews in the country of Palestine started speaking Aramaic when they were taken as slaves by the Babylonian people. Jesus probably spoke Aramaic. (2 Kings 18: 26-28; John 19:20)

Ararat (AIR-uh-rat) is a group of mountains. It is located in what is now called Turkey and the Soviet Union. Noah's boat landed here after the flood. (Genesis 8:4; 2 Kings 19: 37; Jeremiah 51:27)

Araunah (a-RAW-nah) was a Jebusite who was also called Ornan. He owned a threshing floor. David wanted to buy it so he could build an altar to God there. Araunah offered to give it to David free. But David refused. Read the story to see why he insisted on paying for it. (2 Samuel 24:15-25; 1 Chronicles 21:18-25)

archangel (ark-AYN-jull) is the title of the leader of God's angels. His name is Michael. (1 Thessalonians 4:16; Jude 9)

Areopagus (AIR-ee-OP-uh-gus) is a Greek word that means "Ares' Hill" (or Mars Hill). It was also the name of a council or group of important leaders in Athens. They were like judges. In New Testament times the Areopagus usually met in the city's marketplace. Paul spoke to them about the true God. (Acts 17:19-34)

Aristarchus (air-i-STAR-kus) means "the best ruler." He was a man from Thessalonica who often traveled with Paul. He stayed with Paul during some of his difficult times. He even went to prison with Paul. (Acts 27:2; Colossians 4:10; Philemon 24)

ark, Noah's, (or Noah's boat) is the huge boat that Noah built. It saved his family from the flood God sent to cover the earth. It was at least as long as one and a half football fields.

Noah's ark

There was one door and an opening for air. The Hebrew word for the kind of wood he used is "gopher." This is probably what we call "cypress" wood today. (Genesis 6:9–8:19)

Ark of the Covenant See "Box of the Agreement with the Lord."

Artaxerxes (ar-tah-ZERK-sees) was either the title or the name of Persian kings. This was during the time when Ezra and Nehemiah were rebuilding Jerusalem. (Ezra 4:6-7; 6:14; 7:1-27)

Artemis (AR-tuh-mis) was the name of a goddess that many Greeks worshiped. The Romans called her "Diana." A beautiful temple was built to honor her in Ephesus. Paul preached about the true God in the city of Ephesus. Read the story to see why this made some people angry. (Acts 19:23-41)

Asa (AY-sah) means "healing." He was the third king of Judah. He is one of the kings who tried to stop the people from worshiping false gods. (1 Kings 15:9-24; 2 Chronicles 14–16)

Asaph (AY-saf) means "collector." He was a leader of singers when David was king. His descendants became singers in the Temple. (1 Chronicles 25:1; Psalms 73–83)

ascension (uh-SIN-shun) means "going up" or "lifted up." The word is used to describe Jesus' return to heaven. Forty days after he was raised from death, Jesus was with the apostles on the Mount of Olives. As he was going up to heaven, a cloud hid him from their sight. But two angels said, "He will come back in the same way you saw him go." (Acts 1:2-12; 2:32-33)

Ashdod (ASH-dahd) means "a fort." In the Old Testament it was one of five strong, walled cities of the Philistines. It is called Azotus in the New Testament. (1 Samuel 5:1-7; 6:17; Nehemiah 13:23-24; Acts 8:40)

Asherah (ah-SHIR-ah) was the name of a Canaanite goddess thought to be the wife of the false god Baal. (Judges 3:7; 1 Kings 15:13; 2 Kings 21:7; 2 Chronicles 15:16)

Ashkelon (ASH-keh-lon) was one of the five important cities of the Philistines. It was located on the coast of the Mediterranean Sea. Several nations captured the city at various times. Herod the Great was born there. (Judges 1:18; 14:19; 1 Samuel 6:17; Zephaniah 2:4,7)

Ashtoreth (ASH-toh-reth) was the name of a goddess of the people of Assyria and Canaan. At times the

Ashtoreth

Israelites forgot God and built idols to worship her. This goddess was also called "Astarte." (Judges 2:13; 1 Samuel 7:3; 12:10; 1 Kings 11:5,33)

Asia (AY-zhuh) means "orient" or "Eastern." It was the name of the western part of the country we now call Turkey. Ephesus was its capital. (Acts 20:16; Revelation 1:4)

Assyria (uh-SEER-ee-uh) was a powerful nation north and east of Israel. Its two most important cities were Nineveh and Ashur. Assyria controlled many smaller countries around it. Assyria attacked Samaria when Hoshea was king. They removed many Israelites from Israel and sent many Assyrians to live in Samaria. The people who were a mixture of Assyrians and Israelites were later called Samaritans. (2 Kings 17:3-6, 24)

Astarte (ah-STAR-tay) was another name for the goddess Ashtoreth. See "Ashtoreth."

Athaliah (ath-uh-LY-uh) was the only woman who ruled over Judah. She was the daughter of Jezebel and Ahab, king of Israel. When her son Ahaziah died, she had many relatives killed so she could become queen. This evil woman was killed after ruling six years. (2 Chronicles 22: 10–23:21)

Athens (ATH-enz) was the "city of Athene." Its name came from the famous Greek goddess Athena. Athens was the leading city of the country of Greece. It was famous as a city of learning and education. The apostle Paul preached in Athens on his second missionary journey. (Acts 17:16,22; 18:1)

Atonement, Day of, See "Cleansing, Day of."

Augustus Caesar (aw-GUS-tus SEE-zer) or Caesar Augustus was the first Roman emperor. He was the ruler when Jesus was born. He was a nephew to the famous Julius Caesar. (Luke 2:1-2)

B

Baal (BA-al) was a false god of the Canaanites. "Baal" was the common word for "master, lord." He was known as the son of Dagon, or the son of El, who was known as the father of the false gods. (1 Kings 18:17-40; Jeremiah 11:13)

Baal-Zebub See "Beelzebul."

Baasha (BAY-ah-shah) became the third king of Israel by killing Nadab and his relatives. He caused the people to sin by leading them to worship false gods. Because of this, God did not allow his descendants to be kings. (1 Kings 15:27–16:7)

Babel, Tower of, is a name given to

a tall building built after the flood. Most Bible scholars believe it was a "ziggurat." A ziggurat is a tower where each story is smaller than the

one below it. The people planned to build a tower so high that its top would reach into the sky. God was not pleased with the Babylonians' plan. So, he confused their languages. Since the workers could no longer understand each other, they had to stop building. (Genesis 11:1-9)

Babylonians (bab-e-LONE-e-unz) were the people from Babylonia. This was a land east of Israel. Their largest city was Babylon. When Nebuchadnezzar was their king, they took many of the people of Judah to Babylonia as captives. The Babylonians were sometimes called Chaldeans. (2 Kings 25:4-26; 2 Chronicles 36; Daniel 1–4)

Balaam (BAY-lum) was a prophet from Midian. He was hired by Balak king of Moab to come and curse the Israelites. On his way God caused Balaam's donkey and an angel to speak to him. Balaam was told to say good things about Israel, not curses. He did this, but later he led some Israelites to serve a false god, Baal. (Numbers 22–24; 31:8,16; 2 Peter 2:15-16)

balm was an oil from a plant used as a medicine to comfort and heal sore skin. (Genesis 37:25; Jeremiah 51:8)

Baptist (BAP-tist) means "someone who baptizes." John, a relative of Jesus, was called this because he baptized many people. (Matthew 3:11)

baptize (BAP-tize) is a Greek word that in New Testament times meant to dip or immerse. Baptism as practiced by Christians was in water. Baptism reminds us of Jesus' death, burial and rising to live again. It shows our death to sin and our being raised to new life with Christ. (Acts 2:38,41; 8:36-39; 10:47; 16:15,33; 18:8; Romans 6:3-4)

B

Word Clues

bar

means "son of" in the Bible. It is often used with a man's name to identify him, such as Simon "Bar-Jonah," who was Simon (or Peter) the son of Jonah (John). Through the years the saying was shortened to "Peter, John's son." Eventually, the name was run together and became the man's last name, "Peter Johnson." What other family names might have come about this way? See Matthew 16:17.

Barabbas (bah-RAB-us) means "son of a father." He was a robber who had murdered someone in Jerusalem. He was in jail when Jesus was on trial. It was the time of year when a criminal would be freed from prison. The people cried out to have Barabbas freed and Jesus killed on the cross. Pilate, the Roman governor, did as they demanded. (Matthew 27:16-26; Mark 15:6-11)

Barak (BAY-rak) means "lightning." He was a leader of Israel's army. When Deborah was judge, she chose Barak to command their army against the Canaanites. God confused the soldiers of Sisera, their enemy, and Barak's men won a great victory. Afterward he and Deborah sang a song to celebrate. (Judges 4–5)

Bar-Jesus See "Elymas."

Barnabas (BAR-nah-bus) means "one who encourages." The apostles gave this name to Joseph because he helped others. Barnabas, who was from Cyprus, often traveled with Paul to teach about Jesus. The journeys of Barnabas with Paul are told in Acts 13–15. (Acts 4:36-37; 11:22-26)

Bartholomew (bar-THOL-oh-mew) was 1 of the 12 apostles of Jesus. He may also have been called Nathanael. (Matthew 10:2-3; Luke 6:13-15; John 1:43-50)

Bartimaeus (bar-teh-MAY-us) means "son of Timaeus." He was a blind man who was healed by Jesus. He was begging for money near Jericho when Jesus came by. Bartimaeus called for help, and Jesus healed him because he showed faith. (Mark 10:46-52)

Baruch (BAH-rook) means "blessed." He was a friend of the prophet Jeremiah. He wrote down the messages that God gave Jeremiah. (Jeremiah 36)

Bathsheba (bath-SHE-buh) means "daughter of the promise." She was the mother of Solomon and wife of David. She had earlier been the wife of Uriah, but David had Uriah killed and married her. The death of their first child was part of God's punishment for that sin. (2 Samuel 11–12; 1 Kings 1–2)

beatitude (bee-A-ti-tyood) means "blessed." This name is often used for Jesus' teaching in Matthew 5:3-12 and Luke 6:20-22. In these verses Jesus described a blessed or happy person.

Beelzebul (bee-EL-ze-bull), also spelled Beelzebub, came from the name Baal-Zebub. This was the name of the false god of the Philistines. In the New Testament, Beelzebul is a name sometimes used for the devil. (Matthew 12:24; Mark 3:22-23)

Beersheba (beer-SHE-buh) means "well of the promise." It is the town

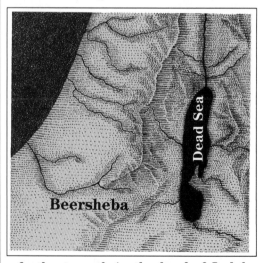

farthest south in the land of Judah. Read the story in Genesis to see how Beersheba got its name. (Genesis 21:22-34; 2 Samuel 3:10)

Bel was a false god of the Babylonians. (Jeremiah 50:2)

believers (be-LEE-vers) is a word used in the New Testament to describe the followers of Jesus. (Acts 2:41-47; 5:14)

Belshazzar (bell-SHAZ-ur) was a ruler of Babylon. God was displeased with his sinful life. During a great banquet, a hand appeared and wrote on the wall. Daniel was called in to tell what the writing meant. The message was that Belshazzar was being punished and his kingdom was about to end. That night the Persian army captured Babylon and Belshazzar was killed. (Daniel 5)

Belteshazzar (BELL-teh-SHAZ-er) was the Babylonian name that Nebuchadnezzar gave to Daniel. (Daniel 4:8,18-19) See also "Daniel."

Benaiah (bee-NAY-uh) was the captain of David's bodyguard. He helped Solomon take David's place as king. Then he became commander of Solomon's army. (2 Samuel 23:20-23; 1 Kings 1–2)

Ben-Hadad (ben-HAY-dad) means "son of Hadad." Hadad was the name the Arameans (or Syrians) gave their storm god. Ben-Hadad was the name (or title) of two or three kings. They often fought against Israel. (1 Kings 20; 2 Kings 6:24–8:15)

Benjamin (BEN-jah-min) was the youngest son of Jacob and Rachel. His mother died when he was born. He and Joseph were his father's favorite sons. King Saul and the apostle Paul were descendants of Benjamin. (Genesis 35:16-21; 42–45)

Bernice (bur-NY-see) was the oldest daughter of Herod Agrippa I. She was married several times and was a very sinful woman. Paul preached to her when she was living with her brother Agrippa. But they did not accept God's message. (Acts 25:13–26:32)

Bethany (BETH-uh-nee) was a small town about two miles from Jerusalem. It was on the road to Jericho. Jesus' friends Mary, Martha and Lazarus lived here. (Matthew 21:17; Mark 14:3; Luke 24:50; John 11)

Bethel (BETH-el) means "house of God." It was a town about 12 miles north of Jerusalem. Jacob named it Bethel because there he had an unusual dream about a ladder reaching to heaven. Many years later Jeroboam built golden calf idols there. (Genesis 28:10-19; Judges 20:26-28; 1 Kings 12:26-30; Amos 3:14)

Bethesda (beth-ES-da) See "Bethzatha, Pool of."

Bethlehem (BETH-le-hem) means "house of bread." It is a small town five miles from Jerusalem in the country of Judea. It was the home town of King David in the Old Testament. Jesus was born there. (1 Samuel 16:4; Matthew 2:1; Luke 2:15-18)

Bethsaida (beth-SAY-ih-duh) means "house of fish." It was a city in Galilee and the home of apostles Peter, Andrew and Philip. (John 1:44; 12:21)

Bethzatha, Pool of, (beth-ZAY-tha) was a pool in Jerusalem near the Sheep Gate. The water came from an underground spring that bubbled up from time to time. People tried to be the first one in the water when it

B

bubbled. They thought the water might heal them. At this pool Jesus healed a man who couldn't walk. (John 5:1-18)

Bible (BY-bul) means "the book." The Bible is a group of books and letters that Christians accept as the word of God. It is divided into two parts. The Old Testament contains 39 books, and the New Testament contains 27 books. See also "Scriptures."

bishop See "elder."

blasphemy (BLAS-feh-mee) is saying things against God. Jesus was often accused of blasphemy because he said he was the Son of God. The people who accused him did not understand that he really was God's Son. (Matthew 9:3; 26:65; John 10:36)

blessing (BLES-ing) is a good gift from God to his people. (Luke 6:28; 24:50-51; Acts 3:26; Hebrews 6:7; 1 Peter 3:9)

body of Christ sometimes means Jesus' human body that suffered and died on the cross. But in some places in the Bible the "body of Christ" is a way of describing Christians. All the parts of a human body work together to do what the mind wants done. In the same way, Christians work together to do what Christ wants. So, the church is called the body of Christ. (Ephesians 1:22-23; 4:15-16; Hebrews 10:10)

bottomless pit is a name sometimes given to the place where those who disobey God are sent when they die. (Revelation 9:1-11; 11:7; 17:8; 20:1-3)

box of Scriptures (also called "phylacteries" or "frontlets") were small leather boxes that some Jews tied to their foreheads and left arms. Inside

they kept copies of Exodus 13:1-16, Deuteronomy 6:4-9 and 11:13-21. Jesus criticized the way some Jews made these boxes larger to show off how religious they were. (Deuteronomy 6:8; Matthew 23:5)

Box of the Agreement with the Lord is often called Ark of the Covenant. It was a special box made of acacia wood and gold. Gold creatures with wings covered the top. Inside were the stone tablets on which the Ten Commandments were written. Later, a pot of manna and Aaron's walking stick were also put into the Box. It was to remind the people of Israel of God's promise to be with them. It is also called the Holy Box of God. (Exodus 25:10-22; 26:34; Joshua 3:1-17; 2 Chronicles 35:3; Hebrews 9:4)

Birds of the Bible

Dove

Sparrow

Stork

Raven

Quail

Vulture

Eagle

Peacock

Owl

Partridge

bread was the most important food in New Testament times. It was usually made of barley or wheat. When made without yeast, it had special meaning for Jews and Christians. Jesus called himself the "bread of life" because he gives real life to his people. (Psalm 104:15; Matthew 4:3; 26:26-28; Mark 8:14; John 6:48-51; 1 Corinthians 11:23-26) See also "unleavened bread."

bread that shows we are in God's presence is also called Bread of the Presence, or showbread. It was a group of 12 loaves of bread that were kept on the table in the Holy Tent and later in the Temple. This special bread reminded the people that they were always in God's presence. (Exodus 25:30; Leviticus 24:5-9; Luke 6:1-4)

brother in the Bible can mean more than just a family member. People from the same country or family group sometimes called each other "brother." Christians use this word to show that they all have the same heavenly father, God. It also means that Christians love each other as brothers in a family. (2 Samuel 19: 12; Acts 9:17; Philemon 16; James 2:15)

Caesar (SEE-zer) was the name of a famous Roman family. In New Testament times it was used as the title of the Roman emperors. (Luke 2:1; 3:1; 20:22-25) See "Augustus Caesar."

Caesarea (SES-uh-REE-uh) was a city named for Augustus Caesar, the first ruler of the Roman Empire. It was built by the Jewish ruler Herod about 20 years before Jesus was born. This city was on the edge of the sea and was the home of Philip the preacher and Cornelius, the first non-Jew to become a Christian. (Acts 10:1; 21:8; 23:31)

Caesarea Philippi (SES-uh-REE-uh fih-LIP-eye) was a city at the base of Mount Hermon, near the beginning of the Jordan River. A ruler called Philip the Tetrarch built this city to honor himself and Augustus Caesar. (Matthew 16:13-20; Mark 8:27-33)

Caiaphas (KAY-uh-fus) was the Jewish high priest from A.D. 18 to 36. He was one of those who planned to kill Jesus. (Matthew 26:57-68; John 11:49-53; 18:12-28)

Cain was the first son of Adam and Eve. He and his brother Abel each gave an offering to the Lord. God was not pleased with Cain's gift, but he was pleased with Abel's gift. Cain became jealous and killed Abel. God punished Cain by making him leave home and wander for the rest of his life. (Genesis 4:1-17; 1 John 3:12)

calamus (KAH-lah-mus) is a sweet-tasting plant stalk probably like sugar cane. (Exodus 30:23; Jeremiah 6:20; Ezekiel 27:19)

Caleb (KAY-leb) was 1 of the 12 spies Moses sent to find out about the promised land of Canaan. Joshua and Caleb were the only ones who thought God would help them take the land. So they were the only adults who were allowed to go into the promised land. (Numbers 13–14; Joshua 14:6-15)

calendar, Jewish, was different from our calendars today. The months had different names, and the year began at a different time. See the illustration on page 22 for how the Jewish calendar compares to ours today.

camel is a useful animal, both today and in Bible times. It has broad, flat feet so it can walk easily on sand and carry heavy loads. A camel can go several days without water. In

camel

Bible times, owning camels was a sign that a person was wealthy.

(Genesis 24:10-64; 1 Samuel 30:17; 2 Kings 8:9; Job 1:3)

Cana (KAY-nah) was a small town near the city of Nazareth in the country of Galilee. Jesus did his first miracle in Cana. There he changed water into wine at a wedding feast. (John 2:1-11; 4:46-54)

Capernaum (kah-PUR-nay-um) was a city on the western shore of Lake Galilee. It was first named the Village of Nahum. Jesus and the apostles often stayed there. Although they did many miracles there, most of the town's people still did not believe in Jesus. (Matthew 4:13; 8:5-17; Luke 4:31-37; 10:15)

capital is the top of a pillar. This top part of the pillar was usually decorated with beautiful carvings. (1 Kings 7:16-20; 2 Kings 25:17; Amos 9:1)

cassia (CASH-ah) is a pleasant-smelling powder. Its odor is like the bark of the cinnamon plant. (Exodus 30:24; Psalm 45:8)

census (SEN-sus) means to count the number of people who live in an area. Moses counted the Israelites before and after the 40 years in the wilderness. Later David counted the people of his kingdom. And Jesus was born in Bethlehem because his parents had to go there to be counted. (Numbers 1:2; 26:2; 1 Chronicles 21:1-7; Luke 2:1-7)

centurion (sin-TUR-ree-un) was a Roman army officer who commanded 100 soldiers. (Matthew 8:5; 7:12)

Cephas (SEE-fuss) is the Aramaic word for "rock." In Greek the word is "Peter." Jesus gave this name to the

THE JEWISH AND MODERN CALENDARS

Jewish Calendar	Our Calendar	Farm season
Abib (Nisan) 1—New Moon 14—Passover 15—Sabbath—holy worship 16—week of unleavened bread 21—holy worship	March/April	later spring rain beginning of barley harvest
Iyyar (Ziv) 1—New Moon	April/May	barley harvest

Sivan
  1—New Moon
  6–7—Feast of Weeks
	May/June	wheat harvest

Tammuz 1—New Moon	June/July	
Ab 1—New Moon	July/August	figs and olives ripen
Elul 1—New Moon	August/September	vintage season
Tishri (Ethanim) 1—New Moon New Year's Day Feast of Trumpets 10—Day of Atonement 15–22—Feast of Tabernacles	September/October	former early rains plowing time
Heshvan 1—New Moon	October/November	seeding time for wheat and barley
Kislev (Chislev) 1—New Moon	November/December	
Tebeth	December/January	
Shebat	January/February	
Adar	February/March	almond trees blossom

centurion

apostle Simon. He became known as Simon Peter. (John 1:42) See also "Peter."

chaff (CHAF) is the husk of a head of grain. Farmers must separate it from the good part of the grain. In Bible times they tossed the grain and chaff together into the air. Since the chaff is lighter, the wind would blow it away and the good grain would fall back to the threshing floor. (Job 21:18; Psalms 1:4; 35:5; Isaiah 29:5; 41:2) See "threshing."

Chaldeans See "Babylonians."

chariot (CHAIR-e-ut) was a fast, two-wheeled cart usually pulled by two horses. It was used for battles, trav-

eling and parades. (Genesis 46:29; Exodus 14:6; Acts 8:28-31)

Chemosh (KEE-mosh) was the name of a false god of the Moabites. (Numbers 21:29; Jeremiah 48:46)

cherubim (CHAIR-uh-bim) are heavenly beings with wings and the faces of men and animals. They guarded the garden of Eden to keep people from getting to the tree of life. Carvings and drawings of cherubim were in the Holy Tent and the Temple. In our Bibles cherubim are sometimes just called "angels" or "creatures with wings." (Genesis 3:24; Exodus 25:18-22; 1 Kings 6:23-35; Ezekiel 10:1-20)

chosen is a word used to describe those who are being saved. God told the Israelites that he had chosen them to be his special people. But it was not because they were greater than everyone else; it was because of God's love. Christians are also chosen people. We have been chosen to tell others of God's love. (Deuteronomy 7:7-8; 9:4-5; Ephesians 1:4-5,11; Colossians 3:12; 1 Peter 2:9-10)

Christ (KRYST) means "anointed (or chosen) one" in Greek. In Hebrew the word is "Messiah." Jesus is the Christ. He was chosen by God to save people from their sins. (Mark 8:29; 14:61-62; Luke 23:2; Acts 2:36; 17:3; 18:28)

Christian (KRIS-chun) means "belonging to Christ." Christ's followers are called Christians. (Acts 11:26; 26:28; 1 Peter 4:16)

Chronicles (KRON-ih-kulz), **First and Second,** are two books in the Old Testament that tell some of the same stories that are in the books of

2 Samuel and 1 and 2 Kings. The Chronicles tell about the kings of the southern kingdom of Judah.

church in the New Testament means a group of Christians. In those times the church often met in someone's home. (Matthew 16:18; Acts 2:47; 14:27; Romans 16:5)

circumcision (SIR-kum-SIH-zhun) means to cut off the foreskin of the male sex organ. Each Jewish baby boy was circumcised on the eighth day after he was born. This act was done as a sign of the agreement God had made with his people, the Jews. Because of this, the Jews sometimes are called "the circumcision" and non-Jews are called "the uncircumcision." (Leviticus 12:3; John 7:22; Acts 7:8)

city of refuge See "safety, city of."

Claudius (CLAW-dee-us) was the fourth Roman emperor. He ruled from A.D. 41 to 54 and gave Jews the right to worship. But Claudius also forced all Jews to leave Rome for a time. This was because they had caused some trouble. (Acts 11: 28; 18:2)

clean is used to describe the state of a person, animal or action that is pleasing to God. God called some animals clean and said they could be eaten. People who had not touched or eaten anything God said was unclean were called clean. Or, if they did not have a disease that made them unclean, they were called clean. They could live and serve God normally. (Genesis 7:2; Leviticus 20:25; Deuteronomy 14:3-20) See "unclean."

Cleansing, Day of, is also called the Day of Atonement. It was the most special day of the year for the Israelites. No one worked or ate on that day. This was the one day of the year when the high priest could go into the Most Holy Place. Animals were sacrificed for the sins of the people. This was a sign to the people that they were cleansed from their sins for a year. Jews still celebrate this day today. It is called Yom Kippur. (Leviticus 16:1-34; 25:9)

Word Clues

clear as crystal means something is very plain or obvious. "The answer to the problem is as clear as crystal." It comes from Revelation 4:6 where John describes the area around the throne of God.

Colossae (koh-LAH-see) was a city in the country of Turkey. The book of Colossians in the New Testament is a letter the apostle Paul wrote to the Christians in Colossae. (Colossians 1:1-2)

Colossians (koh-LAH-shunz) is a letter written by Paul to the church at Colossae. He wrote it about A.D. 61, while he was in prison. Some people had been teaching false ideas at Colossae. So, Paul reminded them about how important Jesus is. Then he showed how those who believe in Jesus should live at home, at work and in the church.

communion (KUH-myu-nyun) See "Lord's Supper."

concubine (KON-kyu-bine) See "slave woman."

condemn (kon-DIM) means to judge someone guilty of doing wrong and to state a punishment. All people are sinners and judged guilty by God. But Jesus came to save us from the punishment we deserve. Those who love and obey God are no longer judged guilty. (Psalm 34:21-22; John 3:16-18; Romans 5:16; 8:1,34)

coney See "rock badger."

confess (kun-FES) means to admit that something is true. The New Testament teaches a believer to confess that Jesus is the Son of God. Christians are also told to confess their sins, to admit that they have done wrong. (Romans 10:9-10; Philippians 2:11; 1 John 1:9)

conscience (KON-shunts) is a person's belief about what is right and wrong. The Bible says that we should not do anything we believe is wrong. Instead, we should do what we know is right. (Acts 24:16; Romans 2:15; 1 Corinthians 8:7-12; 1 Timothy 1:5,19; 2 Timothy 1:3)

conversion (kon-VER-zhun) means "turning" or "coming back." It is used to describe a person's turning toward God and becoming a Christian. The book of Acts tells about the conversion of many people. (Acts 3:19; 8:26-39; 9:1-20; 16:11-34)

coral (KOR-al) is a type of limestone that forms in the ocean. Coral is usually a rich red or deep pink color. It is used to make jewelry. (Job 28:18; Ezekiel 27:16)

Corinth (KOR-inth) was a large seaport in the country of Greece. The city was known for the sinful things its people did. Paul wrote the books of 1 and 2 Corinthians as letters to the Christians in Corinth. He told them how they should live. (Acts 18:1-11; 1 and 2 Corinthians)

Corinthians (ko-RIN-thee-enz) are two letters that Paul wrote to the church at Corinth. In the first letter he answers some questions the people had asked him. In 2 Corinthians Paul explains about his being an apostle and how he feels about the Corinthian church.

Cornelius (kor-NEEL-yus) was a Roman army officer in charge of 100 soldiers. He worked with the army in the city of Caesarea. He was a man of good works who helped the poor. Cornelius, his family and some of his friends were the first non-Jewish people to become Christians. (Acts 10)

cornerstone This was the most important stone at a corner in the base of a building. The cornerstone had to be perfect so the building's walls would be straight. The other stones were fitted against the cornerstone. Jesus is called the cornerstone of the new law. (Joshua 6:26; Job 38:6; Ephesians 2:20)

council (KOWN-s'l), or meeting, was the highest Jewish court in the days of Jesus. Its proper name was the "Sanhedrin." The men of the council sat in a half-circle to hear the people who came to speak to them. The trials of Jesus and Stephen were held in front of this council. (Matthew 26:57-68; Acts 6:13-15)

court, courtyard is a part of a building that has walls, but no roof. In Bible times the Temple had four of these courts.

The Court of the Non-Jews (Gentiles) was a large open area inside the walls of Herod's Temple. Anyone could come in. The money-

courtyard

changers were here when Jesus forced them out. (Mark 11:15-17; John 10:23; Acts 3:11)

The Court of Women was an area where both men and women were allowed. Jesus was here when he saw the poor widow give the last of her money. (Mark 12:41-44)

The Court of Israel was the next inner part of the Temple. Only Jewish men were allowed here.

The Court of the Priests was the innermost court in the Temple. Only the priests were allowed here. (Matthew 23:35)

covenant (KUV-eh-nant) See "agreement."

covet (KUV-et) means to want strongly something that belongs to someone else. The Bible says this is wrong. When a person covets, he is not trusting enough in God to care for him. (Exodus 20:17; Joshua 7:20-21; Colossians 3:5; Hebrews 13:5)

creation (kre-AY-shun) means that God made the world and all of the universe. People and all of nature were made as a part of God's plan. God continues to keep the world working. (Genesis 1—2; Job 38—41; Psalms 8,103; Isaiah 40:21-26; John 1:1-3; Hebrews 11:3)

Crete (KREET) is an island in the Mediterranean Sea. It is south of the country of Greece. Paul and Titus began a church there. (Acts 27:7-13; Titus 1:5)

cross refers to a cruel way of killing criminals in New Testament times. The person was tied or nailed to two rough beams of wood nailed together in the shape of an "x" or a "t." Then, he was left hanging in a public place

cross

to die. Jesus was killed by the Roman soldiers this way. In the New Testament the word "cross" is often used to remind us that Christ's death on the cross was God's way of saving us from our sins. (John 19:17-31; 1 Corinthians 1:18-25; Galatians 6:12; Ephesians 2:15-16)

crown is a special band worn around the head. A king wears a crown to show that he is the ruler. A crown is usually made of gold. An athlete in New Testament times received a crown of leaves for winning his contest. The Bible says our reward in heaven is like receiving the athlete's victory crown. (2 Samuel 12:29-30; 1 Corinthians 9:25; 2 Timothy 4:8; 1 Peter 5:4)

crucifixion (kroo-suh-FIK-shun) See "cross."

cubit (KU-bit) was an important measurement in Bible times. A cubit was the length of a person's arm from the point of the elbow to the end of the middle finger, usually about 18 inches.

cud An animal that "chews the cud" chews its food slightly and swallows it. Then it chews it more completely a second time. (Leviticus 11:3)

cupbearer is a name for the officer who tasted and served the king his wine. Only a very trusted person was given this job. (Genesis 40:1,21; 41:9; Nehemiah 1:11)

curse means to say that you wish something terrible would happen to someone. (Matthew 15:4; Mark 14:71; John 7:49)

Cush means "black." It was the name of a country in Africa, just south of Egypt. It is called Ethiopia today. (Genesis 2:13; Psalm 68:31; Isaiah 18:1)

crown

Cyprus (SY-prus) is an island in the Mediterranean Sea. It was the home of Barnabas. He and Paul began a church there. (Acts 4:36; 13:4; 15:39)

Cyrene (sy-REE-nee) was a city in North Africa (west of Egypt). It is in Libya today. Many Jews and Greeks lived there. A man named Simon from Cyrene was visiting in Jerusalem when Jesus was killed. This Simon was forced by the Roman soldiers to carry the cross for Jesus. (Matthew 27:32; Acts 2:10; 6:9)

Cyrus (SY-rus) was a king of Persia. He captured Babylonia in 539 B.C. Cyrus was the one who let the Jews who were in captivity return to Jerusalem. The treasures that Nebuchadnezzar had stolen from the Temple were even returned. Daniel's last years were during Cyrus' rule. (Ezra 1, 6; Isaiah 44:28–45:13)

D

Dagon

Dagon (DAY-gon) was one of the false gods of the Philistines. (Judges 16: 23; 1 Samuel 5:2-7; 1 Chronicles 10:10)

Damascus (duh-MAS-kus) is one of the world's oldest cities. It is about 50 miles east of Lake Galilee in the country of Syria. It is still a very important city today. Saul was on the road to Damascus when Jesus appeared to him. (Acts 9:1-20; 26:20)

Dan was 1 of the 12 sons of Jacob. He was head of 1 of the tribes of Israel. There was also a town named Dan. The Bible often says "from Dan to Beersheba." This meant the whole land of Israel, since Beersheba was the town farthest south and Dan was the city farthest north. (Joshua 19:47-48; Judges 20: 1; 1 Samuel 3:20; 1 Kings 12:29-30)

Daniel (DAN-yel) was a Hebrew captive taken to Babylon as a young man. He told Nebuchadnezzar what one of his dreams meant. God also made him able to tell Belshazzar what the strange handwriting on the wall meant. When he was about 80 years old, Daniel was put in the lions' den by King Darius. But God saved him. (Daniel 1–6)

Daniel, book of, is one of the books of

prophecy in the Old Testament. The first half of the book tells what happened to Daniel and his friends as captives of the Babylonians and Persians. The last half of the book describes Daniel's visions about what would happen in the future.

Darius (dah-RYE-us) was the name of at least two rulers of Persia:

Darius Hystaspes (dah-RYE-us his-TAHS-peez) allowed the Jews to finish rebuilding the Temple. The work had been stopped for awhile. When Darius found out that Cyrus had allowed them to start rebuilding, he let them continue. (Ezra 5–6)

Darius the Mede was the king who made Daniel an important ruler under him. He had to put Daniel into the lion's den, even though he didn't want to do it. (Daniel 6)

David (DAY-vid) was Israel's greatest king. Jesus is called the "Son of David" because he was born to members of David's family. (1 Samuel 1:16-31; Luke 1:69; 2:4; 18:38; Acts 2:29-31; 13:22)

Day of Atonement See "Cleansing, Day of."

deacon (DEE-kun) is a Greek word meaning "servant." Deacons are people chosen to serve the church in special ways. The men named in Acts 6:1-6 may have been the first deacons. Deacons are described in 1 Timothy 3:8-13.

Dead Sea is a large lake at the south end of the Jordan River. The Jordan and several small streams flow into it. But it has no outlet. And it is so salty that nothing lives in it. It is about 50 miles long and 10 miles

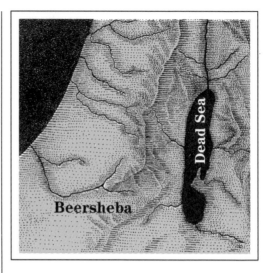

wide. In Bible days it was often called the Salt Sea, the Eastern Sea or the Sea of Arabah. (Genesis 14:3; Numbers 34:3,12; Joshua 3:16)

death is when our physical body stops working. The Bible also talks about spiritual death. That means being separated from God. But Jesus died to solve the problems of both physical and spiritual death. Though our bodies will die, when Jesus returns, they will be changed into new bodies. Our heavenly bodies will never wear out. (Genesis 2:16-17; Romans 6:23; 1 Corinthians 15:21, 26, 35-58; 2 Corinthians 5:1-10; Hebrews 2:14-15)

Deborah (DEB-oh-rah) was the only woman judge over Israel. A Canaanite king named Jabin and his army commander, Sisera, were cruel to the Israelites for 20 years. So, Deborah asked Barak to lead Israel's army against Sisera. God helped the Israelites win, even though Sisera had 900 iron chariots. After the victory Deborah and Barak sang a song about it. (Judges 4–5)

Word Clues

deca

means "ten." It can be combined with other words in Greek to form compound words, such as "decapolis," which means "ten cities." What other words can you think of that contain "deca"?

Decapolis (dee-KAP-oh-lis) means "ten towns." These ten towns were in an area south and mostly east of Lake Galilee. Many of the people in these ten towns were Greeks. Jesus preached and healed here. (Matthew 4:25; Mark 5:20; 7:31)

Delilah (dee-LYE-luh) was an evil Philistine woman whom Samson loved. The Philistines paid her to find out the secret of Samson's strength. She kept bothering him until he finally told her. When she found out that it was his hair, she cut it while he was asleep. In this way he broke his promise to God, lost his strength and was captured. (Judges 16:4-20)

Demas (DEE-mus) was a Christian who helped the apostle Paul when Paul was in prison. But later Demas left Paul. Paul said it was because Demas "loved this world too much." (Colossians 4:14; Philemon 24; 2 Timothy 4:10)

Demetrius (deh-MEE-tree-us) was a silver worker in Ephesus. He made silver statues of false gods. But Paul came preaching about the true God. Demetrius was afraid people would stop buying his idols. So, he got other silver workers to help him start a riot against Paul. (Acts 19: 23-41)

demon (DEE-mun) is an evil spirit from the devil. Sometimes a demon lived in a person. But Jesus has more power than demons and could make them come out of people. (Deuteronomy 32:17; Psalm 106:37; Matthew 12:22; Luke 8:26-39)

descendants (de-SIN-dants) are family members who are born to a person or his children. They would include grandchildren, great-grandchildren, great-great-grandchildren and so on. (Genesis 12:7; Leviticus 21:21; Romans 4:18)

DISTANCES

Orgyia (or fathom) = 6 feet

Stadion (or furlong) = 202 yards

Mile (or milion) = 1,000 paces or 1,618 yards

Sabbath Day's Journey was the maximum distance allowed by the Jewish law. It was set at 2,000 cubits or 1,000 yards.

A little way probably meant a definite distance, but it's not certain how far. It may have been about 30 furlongs or 4 miles.

Day's Journey was not an exact distance. The ordinary day's journey among the Jews was 20 to 30 miles. But if a group traveled together, it was only 10 miles.

Deuteronomy (DOO-ter-OHN-oh-mee) means "second law." It is the name of the fifth book of the Old Testament, which gives new laws and explains older ones. It is mainly the speeches Moses gave before Israel went into the promised land. The last chapter tells how Moses died.

Read it to see what was unusual about his death. (Deuteronomy 34)

devil (DEV-'l) means "one who accuses." In the New Testament, the devil is often called Satan or Beelzebul. He is a spirit and the enemy of God and man. (Matthew 4:1-11; John 13:2; Ephesians 4:27; 6:10-17) See "Beelzebul."

Didymus (DID-ee-mus) means "twin." It was another name for Thomas, 1 of Jesus' 12 apostles. (John 11:16; 20:24; 21:2)

disciple (dih-SYE-p'l) See "follower."

Dorcas (DOR-kus) means "deer." She was also called Tabitha. She was a Christian woman known for helping the poor by making clothes for them. When she died, Christians brought Peter to Joppa where she had lived. He raised her from death. (Acts 9:36-43)

dreams were used by God several times in the Bible to tell people something important. Sometimes he gave someone (like Joseph) the ability to tell what a dream meant. (Genesis 28:12; 37:5-11; 40–41; 1 Kings 3:5-15; Daniel 2; 4; Matthew 1:20; 2:12-22)

Word Clues

drop in a bucket
means a small, unimportant amount. A drop is a very small amount of water compared to how much a whole bucket will hold. It comes from Isaiah 40:15 where Isaiah shows how unimportant the nations are compared to God himself.

E

eagle

eagle is a bird known for its speed and strength. Eagles are often mentioned in the Bible to help us understand important ideas. For example, God told the Israelites that he took them out of Egypt as an eagle carries her young on her wings out of danger. Proverbs says that money can disappear as fast as an eagle flies away. (Exodus 19:4; Deuteronomy 28:49; Job 39:27-30; Proverbs 23:5; 30:18-19; Isaiah 40:31)

earthquake is the moving or shaking

of part of the earth, which sometimes causes large cracks in the earth. God used an earthquake to get Paul and Silas out of prison. (1 Kings 19:11-12; Amos 1:1; Matthew 27:51; 28:2; Acts 16:26)

Ebal (EE-buhl) is a mountain in Samaria next to Mount Gerizim. Once Joshua had the Israelites stand on the two mountains. Then he read to them the law God had given them. The well where Jesus met a Samaritan woman was near Mount Ebal. (Deuteronomy 27:4-8; Joshua 8:30-35; John 4:20)

Ecclesiastes (ee-KLEE-zee-AS-teez) means "teacher." It is the name of one of the Old Testament books of poetry (or wisdom). It seems to have been written by Solomon. He tells some of the lessons that he learned in life. Some of the book is sad and hard to understand. But he ends by saying, "Honor God and obey his commands. This is the most important thing people can do." (Ecclesiastes 12:13)

Eden, garden of, (EE-den) was the home God created for Adam and Eve. It was a place of beauty and peace. The Bible tells us the garden of Eden was near the Tigris and Euphrates rivers. But that covers a large area. So the exact location of the garden is not known. (Genesis 2:8–3:24; Isaiah 51:3; Ezekiel 28:13)

Edom (EE-dum) means "red." Edom, who was also called Esau, was the older son of Isaac. The land where Esau's descendants lived was named Edom. It was south of the Dead Sea. Seir is another name for the land of Edom. (Genesis 25:30; 36:8; 2 Samuel 8:14; Psalm 137:7; Ezekiel 25:12-14; Obadiah 10–14)

Eglon (EGG-lon) was a king of Moab. The Bible says he was very fat. The Lord allowed him to defeat Israel because of their sins. But later the Israelites asked God for help. So, he sent Ehud to be a judge and kill the evil Eglon. (Judges 3:12-25)

Egypt (EE-jipt) is a country in the northeast part of Africa. It is the land of the famous Nile River. In the Old Testament, Moses led the Israelites out of Egypt where they had

been slaves. Later, Mary and Joseph took the baby Jesus to Egypt to keep Herod from killing him. (Genesis 12:10; 50:22; Exodus 1:8; Matthew 2:13-15; Acts 7:9-40; 13:17)

Ehud (EE-hud) was the second judge of Israel. God sent him to save the people from Eglon, the king of Moab, who was forcing Israel to pay him large amounts of money. When Ehud brought the money, he killed Eglon. After that, Israel had many years of peace with Ehud as judge. (Judges 3:12-30)

Word Clues

el

is a Hebrew word that means "God." So, a word with "el" at the beginning or end usually has something to do with God. For instance, "Bethel" means "house of God." "El-Shaddai" means "God-All Powerful." What other Old Testament words can you think of that have "el" as a part of them?

---

elder (EL-der) means "older." In the Old Testament, elders (older leaders) were a special group of men who led God's people. In the New Testament, elders are appointed leaders in the church. (Numbers 11:16; Acts 20:17-38; 1 Timothy 3:1-7; 1 Peter 5:1-4)

election See "chosen."

Eli (EE-lye) was a priest and the next-to-last judge of Israel. Both of Eli's sons became evil men. So, Eli trained young Samuel to take his place. When Eli heard about the death of his two sons, he fell backward off his chair and also died. (1 Samuel 1:9–4:18)

Elihu (ee-LYE-hew) was the fourth one of Job's friends to try to explain why Job was having trouble. He was not as mistaken as Job's first three friends had been, but he still did not completely understand why all the bad things had happened to Job. (Job 32–37)

Elijah (ee-LIE-juh) was a man who spoke for God in the Old Testament. He was a prophet about 800 years before Jesus was born. (1 Kings 17–21; 2 Kings 1–2; Matthew 16:14; 17:3-4; 27:47; Luke 1:17; James 5:17)

Elisha (ee-LYE-shuh) was the prophet who took Elijah's place as God's messenger. He gave God's message to the people for more than 50 years. God gave him the power to do several miracles. He healed sickness, raised people from death, and once made an axhead float. Even after he died, God used Elisha's body as an unusual sign. Read 2 Kings 13:20-21 to find out about it. (2 Kings 2–9; 13:14-21)

Elizabeth (ee-LIZ-uh-beth) was the wife of Zechariah, a priest. She was the mother of John the Baptist. She may have also been a cousin to Mary, the mother of Jesus. (Luke 1:5-45,57-66)

Elkanah (el-KAY-nuh) was the father of Samuel. He had two wives, Hannah and Peninnah. Hannah did not have any children for a long time. But one time, after she prayed very hard at the Holy Tent, the priest Eli told her she would have a child. Hannah had a baby boy whom they named Samuel. Elkanah and Hannah agreed that their son Samuel should be taken to the Holy Tent to be raised by Eli. (1 Samuel 1–2)

Elymas (EL-ih-mus) means "a wise man." He was also called Bar-Jesus. Elymas was a magician in the city of Paphos on the island of Cyprus. He tried to stop Paul and Barnabas from teaching the governor of the island about Jesus. So the Lord made Elymas blind for a while. Then the governor believed and became a Christian. (Acts 13:4-12)

Emmaus (ee-MAY-us) was the name

E

of a town seven miles from Jerusalem. Two of Jesus' followers were walking to Emmaus after he was raised from death. Jesus joined them on the road, but at first they did not recognize him. After they got to Emmaus and were eating, they were allowed to recognize him. Read the story and see what happened to Jesus when they recognized him. (Luke 24:13-39)

endurance See "patience."

Enoch (EE-nok) was a man who lived in the time between Adam and Noah. He was one of the two men who did not die. (The other was Elijah). Enoch loved and obeyed God so well that one day God just took him to heaven. (Genesis 5:21-24; Hebrews 11:5)

enrollment See "census."

envy See "jealous."

Epaphras (EP-ah-fruhs) was a Christian who started the church at Colossae. He visited Paul in prison at Rome. Hearing Epaphras' news about Colossae made Paul want to write the letter to the Colossians. (Colossians 1:7-8; 4:12-13; Philemon 23)

Epaphroditus (ee-PAF-ro-DYE-tus) was a Christian in the church at Philippi. The Philippians sent him to help Paul in prison. There Epaphroditus became seriously ill. When he got well, Paul sent him back with the letter to the Philippians. (Philippians 2:25-30; 4:18)

ephah (EE-fah) was a common measurement for dry materials such as grain. It contained ten omers, about three pecks and three pints. (Exodus 16:36)

ephah

Ephesians (ee-FEE-shunz) is a letter Paul wrote to the church at Ephesus (and probably to other churches in that area, as well). He teaches about God's plan since creation and how Christians should be united. The last two chapters tell how husbands, wives and children should act. The letter ends by showing how to fight against the devil.

Ephesus (EF-eh-sus) was the capital city in the Roman state of Asia. Paul preached in Ephesus for about two years. (Acts 18:19-21,24-28; 19:1; 20:17)

ephod (EF-ahd) See "vest, holy."

Ephraim (EE-frah-im) means "fruitful." He was Joseph's younger son. His descendants were 1 of the 12 tribes of Israel. Joshua was from this tribe. Because Ephraim was an important tribe, the northern kingdom of Israel was sometimes called Ephraim. (Genesis 41:50-52; 48:8-20; Isaiah 7:2)

epistle (e-PIS-'l) is a Greek word meaning "letter." Many books of the New Testament were actually letters written to Christians in various cities. (Colossians 4:16; 1 Thessalonians 5:27)

Esau (E-saw) See "Edom."

Esther (ES-ter) was a Jewish girl who became wife of Ahasuerus, king of Persia. She found out that Haman, the king's most important assistant, was planning to kill all the Jews. So, she risked her own life to save her people. (Esther 1–10)

eternal life is the new kind of life promised to those who follow Jesus. It is living with a new help from God. It is also life that will never end. (John 3:16; 4:14; Galatians 2: 20; 1 John 5:11-15)

Ethiopia See "Cush."

eunuch (YOU-nuk) is a man who cannot have sexual relations. In the Bible, eunuchs were often high officers in royal palaces or armies. (2 Kings 9:32; Esther 2:3; Isaiah 56: 3-5; Acts 8:26-40)

Euphrates (you-FRAY-teez) is a long, important river in Bible lands. It

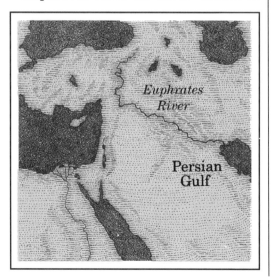

Euphrates River

Persian Gulf

starts in the mountains of Turkey and flows 1,780 miles to the Persian Gulf. It was one of the four rivers in the garden of Eden. God promised that Abraham's descendants would have the land all the way to the Euphrates. Sometimes it is just called "the river" or "the great river" in the Bible. (Genesis 15:18; Deuteronomy 1:7; 2 Samuel 8:3; 1 Kings 4:21)

Eutychus (YOU-ti-cus) means "lucky." Eutychus was a young man in the city of Troas. As he was sitting in an upstairs window listening to Paul preach, he went to sleep. He fell out of the window and died. But Paul, by God's power, brought him back to life. (Acts 20:7-12)

evangelist (ee-VAN-juh-list) is a Greek word that means "someone who tells the Good News." (Acts 21:8; Ephesians 4:11; 2 Timothy 4:5) See also "Good News."

Eve (EEV) means "mother of all living." She was the first woman God made. He made her from a rib which he took from Adam, the first man. (Genesis 2:18-24; 2 Corinthians 11:3; 1 Timothy 2:13-14)

evil spirit See "demon."

Exodus means "going out." The book of Exodus tells about the Israelites going out of Egypt. The first half of the book takes them from Egypt to Mount Sinai. The last half is about the laws God gave them at Sinai.

Ezekiel (ee-ZEEK-yel) was a prophet when the Jews were captured by the Babylonians. He had lived in Jerusalem before being taken to Babylon by Nebuchadnezzar in 597 B.C. There he wrote the book of Ezekiel. In it he told the people to change

E

their hearts and lives. Their sins had caused them to be punished. But the later chapters of his book give some happier news. God tells Ezekiel that the Jews will be allowed to return to Jerusalem and rebuild it.

Ezra (EZ-ra) was the leader of a group of Israelites who were allowed to return to Jerusalem from Babylon. He taught them to worship and serve God correctly. (Ezra 7–10; Nehemiah 8–9)

F

faith (FAYTH) is belief and trust. People who have great faith in God do what he says to do, even when they do not understand why. They do it because they believe in him and trust him. Faith in Jesus means believing he is the Son of God and trusting in him. (2 Chronicles 20:20; Isaiah 7:9; Habakkuk 2:4; Matthew 8:10; Luke 8:24-25; Romans 4:16-22; 5:1-2; Ephesians 4:13; Hebrews 11)

fall is a word sometimes used to describe the first sin. Adam and Eve were created to live happily in the garden of Eden and be close to God. But they listened to Satan and disobeyed God. So, they "fell" from their closeness to God. And since then every person (except Jesus) has also sinned and "fallen" away from God. But Jesus came and died to bring us back into closeness with God. (Genesis 3; Romans 3:22-26; 5:12-21)

famine (FAM-un) means a time of hunger when there is very little food. A famine is caused by such things as not enough rain, too many insects that eat the crops or crops being destroyed by war. There were famines during the lives of Abraham, Joseph, Ruth, David and Elijah. (Genesis 12:10; 41:27-54; Ruth 1:1; 2 Samuel 21:1; 1 Kings 18)

farmer's year See illustration on page 37.

fasting (FAST-ing) means giving up food for a while. People sometimes fast during a special time of prayer and worship to God. Jesus fasted for 40 days before he began preaching. Fasting was also done to show sadness. (2 Samuel 12:16-22; Ezra 8:23; Matthew 4:1-11; 6:16-18; 9:14-15; Acts 12:2-3; 14:23)

Word Clues

fat of the land
means the riches of the country. "He's living off the fat of the land." It comes from Genesis 45:18. There Pharaoh invited Joseph and his family to live in the best part of Egypt and enjoy the riches of the land.

Farmer's Year

Sowing

Harvesting

Threshing

Winnowing

fathom (FATH-um) is a measurement often used to determine the depth of water. It was generally the length of outstretched arms. Today a fathom is six feet. (Acts 27:28)

feast (FEEST) is a special meal and celebration for a certain purpose. There were many different feasts in Bible times.

Feast of Dedication was an eight-day celebration for the Jews. It was a way of being thankful that the Temple had been cleansed again. This was done in 164 B.C. after the Greeks had spoiled and ruined it. The celebration is called Hanukkah today by the Jews. (John 10:22)

Feast of Harvest See "Feast of Weeks."

Feast of Purim (PURE-rim) reminded the Israelites of how they were saved from death during the time of Queen Esther. They read the book of Esther, sang and gave gifts. It is still celebrated today by the Jews for two days in March. (Esther 9:18-32) See also "New Moon."

Feast of Shelters is also called the Feast of Booths or Feast of Tabernacles. The people gathered fruit

and lived in tentlike shelters for a week. This feast reminded them of how God had taken care of them when the Israelites left Egypt and lived in tents in the wilderness. (Exodus 23:14-17; Deuteronomy 16:13-17)

Feast of Unleavened Bread was also called Passover. It was held to help the Israelites remember how God helped them in Egypt. He saved them from the one that brings death that passed over their families. And God led them out of slavery. For seven days they ate bread made without yeast and did only certain types of work. (Exodus 12:14-20; Numbers 28:16-25; Deuteronomy 16:1-8) See "Passover."

Feast of Weeks was also called Pentecost, the Feast of Harvest and the Day of Firstfruits. It was held seven weeks and one day after Passover. This was a feast of thanksgiving for the summer harvest. (Exodus 34:22; Leviticus 23:15-22; Numbers 28:26-31; Deuteronomy 16:9-12; Acts 2) See "Pentecost."

Felix (FEE-lix) was the Roman governor of Judea from A.D. 52 to 54. He was a cruel ruler. He kept the apostle Paul in prison for two years to please the Jews who hated Jesus and Paul. His full name was Marcus Antonius Felix. (Acts 23:24–24:27)

fellowship (FEL-o-ship) is sharing friendship and love with others. Christians have a very special fellowship with God and his people. (Acts 2:42; 1 John 1:3-7)

Festus (FES-tus) was the governor of Judea after Felix. His full name was Porcius (POR-shus) Festus. He allowed Paul to go to Rome to be tried by Caesar. (Acts 24:27–25:27; 26:24-32)

fire was used by God as a sign of his presence and power. God spoke to Moses out of a burning bush. He appeared as a pillar of fire in the wilderness. God also used fire as a way of describing his punishment for evil. (Exodus 3:1-6; 13:21; 24:17; Matthew 18:8; Hebrews 12:28-29; 2 Peter 3:7-12; Revelation 19:20)

firstborn (FIRST-born) is the oldest child in a family. The son born first to a Jewish family received a double share of his father's wealth. Then he became the leader of the family when his father died. The Israelite people were called God's firstborn because he gave them special privileges. Jesus was also called God's firstborn son. He is now ruling over all creation. (Genesis 35:23; Exodus 4:22; Psalm 89:27; Romans 8:29; Colossians 1:18; Hebrews 1:6)

firstfruits (FIRST-fruits) were the first and best crops and animals the Israelites raised and gave to God at harvest time. This showed that they knew everything really belonged to God. (Exodus 34:22-26; Leviticus 23:9-21; Numbers 28:26; Deuteronomy 18:4)

fish was an important food in Bible times. Many kinds of fish lived in Lake Galilee. But Jews were not to eat those kinds of fish without fins or scales (like shellfish or catfish). Much fishing was done at night by the light of a torch. The light attracted the fish, and they were caught with a net. At least seven of Jesus' twelve apostles were fishermen. (Deuteronomy 14:9-10; Matthew 13:47-50; Luke 5:1-7; John 21: 1-13)

flax (FLAKS) is a plant used to make clothing and ropes. The inside of the plant is combed and spun into

thread. Then it is woven into cloth. (Exodus 9:31; Joshua 2:6; Proverbs 31:13; Isaiah 19:9)

flood is a covering of the earth with water. God flooded the whole earth as a punishment because so many people had become evil. Only eight people (Noah and his family) were allowed to enter a boat to be saved. This may have been the first time it had ever rained. Before that the earth may have been watered by a mist that came up from the ground. The waters of the flood came from the sky and underground springs. The rain lasted for forty days. But it was more than a year before it was dry enough for Noah's family to come out of the boat. When they did, God showed them the rainbow. This was his sign that he would never again destroy the earth by water.

(Genesis 6–8; Hebrews 11:7; 2 Peter 3:5-7) See also "ark, Noah's" and "rainbow."

follower (FAHL-o-wer) is a person who is learning from someone. Jesus' followers are those who believe and obey his teaching. Another word for "follower" is "disciple." During his ministry, Jesus chose 12 special followers and made them his apostles. (Matthew 15:32-39; John 19:38; Acts 6:1-7; 11:26)

fool is someone who is not wise. A fool does not understand what is really important in life. (Proverbs 10:8-23; 17:7-28; 26:1-12; Matthew 7:24-26; 25:1-13; Luke 11:37-40; Romans 1: 21-22)

footwashing was necessary in Bible times because people wore sandals. The roads were not paved, but dusty. So, people's feet got very dirty. A servant usually washed the feet of

those who came to a house. Jesus used the custom of footwashing to teach his apostles a lesson about being a servant. (1 Samuel 25:41; Luke 7:44; John 13:4-17; Acts 13:25)

forgiveness (for-GIV-ness) means to be pardoned and not punished for doing a wrong thing. A sinner who is sorry for his sin and stops doing that sin will be forgiven when he comes to God. That person will not be punished. Christians are also to

F

forgive others for wrong things done to them. (Genesis 50:17; Psalms 19:12; 32:1-5; 51:1-17; Matthew 6:12-15; 9:2-8; 18:21-22; Acts 8:22; Romans 4:7; 1 John 1:9)

fornication (for-ni-KAY-shun) is having sexual relations with someone to whom you are not married. (Genesis 38:24; Deuteronomy 22:20-21) See "adultery."

fountain See "spring."

frankincense (FRANK-in-senz) is a very expensive, sweet-smelling perfume. It comes from inside the tere-

binth tree that grows in the country of Arabia. Some wise men gave frankincense to Jesus when he was born. (Exodus 30:34; Matthew 2:11; Revelation 18:13)

friend is someone who shows love and respect to another person. Jesus often stayed in the home of three of his friends—Mary, Martha and Lazarus. (Proverbs 17:17; 18:24; John 11:33-36; 15:13-15; Acts 10:24; James 2:23)

frontlet See "box of Scriptures."

fruits of various kinds were important foods in Bible lands. The most common fruits were grapes, dates, pomegranates and figs. When the Israelites went into the promised land they found grapes growing in such huge bunches that it took two men to carry one bunch of grapes. When they were in Egypt they had melons to eat, but there is no mention of them after that time. (Numbers 11:5; 13:23; 1 Samuel 25:18; 2 Samuel 6:19; Mark 11:14) See page 41.

fulfill means "to give the full meaning" or "to cause something to come true." Many things had been told about Jesus by the prophets long before he was born. For example, the Jews expected the Christ (Jesus) to be born in Bethlehem because of what the prophet Micah had said. When these things happened, they "fulfilled" the prophets' words by proving them to be true. (Micah 5:2; Matthew 2:4-6; 21:4-5; 27:9; Luke 4:16-21; 24:44-46; John 12:37-41; 19:24)

furnace was a box made of brick or stone. A fire was built inside. These

furnace

Fruits of the Bible

Almond

Date Palm

Fig

Olive

Pomegranate

Vine

furnaces were used for baking pottery and brick or for working with metals like gold, silver and iron. Daniel's three friends were protected by God when they were put in the fiery furnace. Jesus said that hell will be like a blazing furnace. (Proverbs 17:3; Daniel 3:6-30; Matthew 13:42,50)

G

Gabriel (GAY-bree-el) is God's angel who announced that John the Baptist and Jesus would be born. (Luke 1:11-20,26-35)

Gad means "fortune." There were three men named Gad in the Bible:

Gad was the seventh of Jacob's 12 sons. His descendants became the tribe of Gad or the Gadites. The land of the Gadites was on the east side of the Jordan River. (Genesis 30:9-11; Numbers 32; 1 Samuel 13:6-7; 1 Chronicles 12:8-15)

Gad was also the name of a prophet during the time of David. He helped save David's life, and he was not afraid to tell David when David did wrong. (1 Samuel 22:5; 2 Samuel 24:11-18)

Gad was also a writer and musician who helped with the Temple music. (2 Chronicles 29:25-29)

Gadarenes (gad-uh-REENZ) were the people who lived in Gadara, which was southeast of Lake Galilee. Jesus forced demons out of two men there. He sent the demons into a herd of pigs. Read the story to see why this made the Gadarenes angry. (Matthew 8:28-34)

Gaius (GAY-yus) is a name that appears several times in the New Testament. All of these may have been different people. But it is also possible that two of these may have been the same person.

Gaius was a Christian from Corinth. Paul the apostle stayed with him, and the church met in his house. (Romans 16:23; 1 Corinthians 1:14)

Gaius was the name of a man who was well known for helping traveling preachers. John wrote the letter called Third John to him. (3 John)

Gaius of Derbe went with Paul from Troas in Macedonia back to Jerusalem. (Acts 20:4)

Gaius of Macedonia traveled with Paul on his third missionary journey. He was captured by the people of Ephesus in A.D. 54. (Acts 19:29)

Galatia (guh-LAY-shuh) was a district of Asia (now the country of Turkey). Paul preached and began several churches in Galatia. The book of Galatians is a letter Paul wrote to the Christians in Galatia. (Acts 16:6; 18:23; 1 Corinthians 16:1; Galatians 1:2)

Galatians (guh-LAY-shunz) may have been Paul's first letter in the New Testament. Some Jews in these churches in Galatia were teaching that non-Jews had to obey Old Testament laws to be Christians. Paul wrote to tell them that was not true. The Law of Moses shows people they are sinners, but Christ came so that we can be made right with God through faith and obedience. "The important thing is faith—the kind of faith that works through love." (Galatians 5:6b)

Galilee (GAL-i-lee) was the country between the Jordan River and the Mediterranean Sea. It had lots of water and trees, and the land was good for growing grains like wheat and barley. Jesus grew up in the city of Nazareth in Galilee and, so, was often called "the Galilean." (Matthew 4:23-25; 21:11; John 2:1-2; 7: 1,9,41)

Galilee, Lake, (GAL-i-lee) is also called the "Sea of Galilee." It is really a lake 13 miles long and about 8 miles wide. Storms often come up very quickly on this lake. Jesus spent much time around Lake Galilee. (Matthew 4:18-22; 8:23-27; 14:22-36; John 6:1-2,16-21)

Gallio (GAL-ee-oh) was a Roman governor in the country of Achaia. He would not let the Jews punish the apostle Paul. His full name was Junius Annaeus Gallio. (Acts 18: 12-17)

Gamaliel (guh-MAY-lee-el) was a Pharisee and a respected Jewish teacher of the Law of Moses. On one occasion he kept the Jewish leaders in Jerusalem from killing the apostles. The apostle Paul was a student of Gamaliel. (Acts 5:34-40; 22:3)

games, especially athletic contests, were popular among the Greeks in New Testament times. These included boxing, foot races and chariot races. Paul shows how the Christian life is like these contests. Both the Christian and the athlete must be

prepared, follow the rules, concentrate on the goal and finish what he has started in order to win. But the athlete's prize will one day be gone, while the Christian's reward is forever. (1 Corinthians 9:24-27; Galatians 5:7; Philippians 2:16; 3:13-14; 1 Timothy 4:8; 2 Timothy 2:5; 4:7-8; Hebrews 12:1-2)

garden of Eden See "Eden."

garden of Gethsemane See "Gethsemane."

Gath was one of the Philistines' five strong cities. When the Philistines captured the Holy Box, they took it to Gath. The city was also the home of Goliath. David hid in Gath while escaping from King Saul. (Joshua 11:22; 1 Samuel 5; 17:4; 21:10–22:1; 2 Samuel 15:18; 2 Chronicles 26:6)

Gaza (GAY-zuh) was one of the Philistines' five strong cities. This was where Samson was kept in prison and later died. It was an important city on the road to Egypt. So, many nations controlled it at various times. Philip was on the road to Gaza when he met the Ethiopian official. (Judges 16; 1 Samuel 6:17; 2 Kings 18:8; Jeremiah 47; Acts 8:26)

gazelle (gah-ZEL) is an animal of the antelope family. It is known for its

beauty and speed. It is usually about two feet tall and three feet long. (Deuteronomy 12:15,22; 2 Samuel 2:18; Proverbs 6:5)

Gedaliah (ged-uh-LYE-uh) was made governor of Judah by Nebuchadnezzar after capturing Jerusalem. But some of the Jewish army captains killed him after a short rule. (2 Kings 25:22-26; Jeremiah 39:14–41:18)

Gehazi (geh-HAY-zye) was a servant of the prophet Elisha. Once he got some gifts from Naaman by being dishonest. His punishment was to become a leper as Naaman had been. (2 Kings 4:8-37; 5:1-27; 8:1-6)

Gehenna See "Hinnom."

genealogy (jee-nee-AHL-o-jee) is a list of the descendants in a family over a long period of years. The Jews thought genealogies were very important because each family hoped the Messiah (Savior) of the world would be born into his own family. And they knew the Messiah had to be born through the genealogy of King David. The genealogy of Jesus is found in Matthew 1:1-17 and Luke 3:23-28.

Genesis (JEN-eh-sis) means "beginning." It is the name of the first book of the Bible. The first eleven chapters tell of the creation, man's sin, the flood and the beginning of different languages. Chapters 12-50 tell about Abraham and his family. The book ends with the death of Joseph.

Gennesaret, Lake of, See "Galilee, Lake."

Gentiles (JEN-tiles) means "nations." The Jews called anyone who was not a Jew a Gentile. The Jews thought all non-Jewish people were enemies. The Good News of Jesus is for all people, both Jews and non-Jewish people. (Acts 10:44-48; 11:18; 13:46-48; Romans 11:11-13; Ephesians 3:6-8)

Gerasenes (GER-un-seenz), or Gadarenes. See "Gadarenes."

Gerizim (GER-i-zim) is a mountain next to Mount Ebal about 30 miles north of Jerusalem. It was a special mountain to the Samaritans. Their temple was built there. Jacob's well is at the bottom of the mountain. Here Jesus talked about worship with a Samaritan woman. (Deuteronomy 11:29; Joshua 8:33; John 4:20)

Gethsemane (geth-SEM-uh-nee) was a garden of olive trees just outside Jerusalem. It was at the bottom of the Mount of Olives. The night before Jesus was killed, he prayed in this garden. Jesus was there when Judas brought the soldiers to arrest him. (Matthew 26:36-50; Mark 14:32)

giant is a name for a person who is unusually tall and large. A group of giants lived in Canaan before the Israelites came to the land. They were called Nephilim, Rephaites and Ana-

kites. One giant, Og, king of Bashan, slept in a bed that was 13 feet long and 6 feet wide. And Goliath was about 9 feet and 4 inches tall. (Numbers 13:33; Deuteronomy 2:10-11; 3:11; 1 Samuel 17:4; 1 Chronicles 11:23)

Gibeah (GIB-ee-uh) was a city about three miles north of Jerusalem. The Israelites destroyed the city because of a murder that happened there. But it was later rebuilt and was the home of King Saul. (Judges 19:12-14; 1 Samuel 10:26; 22:6)

Gibeon (GIB-ee-uhn) was a town about six miles northwest of Jerusalem. After the Israelites defeated Jericho and Ai, the people of Gibeon were afraid they would be next. So, the Gibeonites tricked the Israelites into not attacking them. Read the story in Joshua 9 to see how they did it. (Joshua 9–10; 2 Samuel 21)

Gideon (GID-ee-uhn) was the judge who led Israel to defeat their enemy the Midianites. God called him to do this job, but he wasn't sure he could do it at first. After God gave him some signs, he agreed to go. The Lord enabled him to win with only 300 men. So, Israel had no more problems with the Midianites for as long as Gideon lived (40 more years). (Judges 6:1–8:35)

Gihon (GYE-hohn) was a spring outside the walls of Jerusalem. Much of the city's water came from the Gihon spring. To keep enemies from cutting off their water supply, King Hezekiah had a tunnel dug through the hill of rock. This brought the spring water into the city to the pool of Siloam. (1 Kings 1:38-39; 2 Chronicles 32:30; 33:14)

Gilead (GIL-ee-ad) was the area that Israel owned on the east side of the Jordan River. This was where the tribes of Reuben, Gad and Manasseh settled to live. Gilead was famous as a good place to raise flocks and herds of animals. (Numbers 32; Deuteronomy 3:10-16)

Gilgal (GIL-gal) was the first place the Israelites camped after crossing the Jordan River into the promised land. As they crossed, they took 12 large stones from the middle of the

G

river. They piled these rocks up at Gilgal. The pile of rocks was to be a reminder for many years. Later children would ask, "What do these rocks mean?" Parents were to tell them how God led his people across the Red Sea and the Jordan River. This would help them to remember God's power and always respect him. Also at Gilgal they ate their first food grown in Canaan. That day the manna stopped coming. (Joshua 4: 1–5:12)

gittith (GIT-tith) is probably a musical word and may be a kind of musical instrument. (Psalms 8; 81; 84)

gleaning is to gather grain left in the

field after harvest. (Ruth 2) See also "farmer's year" and "harvest."

glory means a sign of God's greatness that people could see. The glowing cloud in the wilderness showed God's glory or greatness to the Israelites. The shepherds could see God's glory when the angels told them about Jesus' birth. Peter, James and John also saw God's glory when Jesus' appearance was changed on the mountain. (Exodus 16:10; 24:16-17; 33:18-22; Isaiah 6:1-3; Luke 2:8-14; 9:28-36)

glutton (GLUH-tun) is a person who eats too much. The Bible says gluttony is wrong. (Deuteronomy 21:20; Proverbs 23:20-21; Titus 1:12)

God is the One who made the world and everything in it. He is a spirit and does not have a body as man does. But people can know what God is like because he sent Jesus into the world to show them. God hates evil, but he loves his people so much that he let his Son die for them. God is the wisest and most powerful being in the universe. He has always been alive, and he will always be alive. He is love. Christians are called "children of God" because they have been given a spirit like God. (Genesis 1:1; Psalm 139:7-12; Isaiah 44:6; Matthew 5:9; John 4:24; 14:9; Romans 1:18; 5:8-11; 8:16; 11:36; Hebrews 1:1-4; 1 John 4:7-12)

Word Clues

going and coming
was a military term in Bible days describing how an army was "going out to battle," and hoping they would be "coming back as winners." Somehow through the years the phrase has been turned around, and today we often say, "We don't know whether we're coming or going."

golden calf was the statue Aaron made while Moses was on Mt. Sinai. The Israelites got tired of waiting for Moses to come back with the message from God. So to keep the people happy, Aaron made a calf. He did it by melting the people's gold earrings and then carving the gold into the shape of a calf. He told them this calf was the god who brought them out of Egypt, and they agreed with him. God and Moses were very angry with the people. After the Israelites were punished, Moses asked

Aaron why had he done such a terrible thing. Read the story to see what Aaron's silly answer was. (Exodus 32:1-24) Many years later King Jeroboam made two golden calves for the people to worship. He also caused the people to sin. (1 Kings 12:26-33)

golden rule is what people sometimes call one of Jesus' commands: "Do for other people the same things you want them to do for you." (Matthew 7:12; Luke 6:31)

golgotha (GOL-guh-thuh) is an Aramaic word meaning "skull." The Latin word for it is "calvary." This is the hill where Jesus was killed on the cross by the Roman soldiers. It may have been called "the place of the skull" because many people died there. Or it may have been called that because the hill looks like a giant skull. (Matthew 27:32-35; Mark 15:22-24; John 19:17-18)

Goliath (go-LYE-eth) was the giant from Gath. He was 9 feet 4 inches tall. Goliath was a Philistine who challenged the Israelites to fight, but everyone was afraid of him. Then David heard about the challenge. He said that God would help him win and show who the true God was. David chose five stones to use in his sling, but he knocked Goliath down with the first one. Goliath had a brother who also must have been very large. Later Elhanan, one of David's men, killed the brother, too. (1 Samuel 17; 1 Chronicles 20:5)

Gomorrah (goh-MO-ruh) was a city near Sodom. Both towns had become so evil that not even ten good people could be found there. So, God destroyed both cities by sending burning sulfur from the sky. Some people think that the two cities may now be under the waters of the Dead Sea. (Genesis 18–19; Matthew 10:11-15; 2 Peter 2:6)

Good News is also called the gospel. In the New Testament, the Good News is that Jesus died for us on the cross, was buried in a tomb and came back to life. Because he did these things for us, we can be saved. That is good news. (Mark 1:1; Acts 20:24; Colossians 1:21-23; 2 Timothy 1:10) See "gospel."

gopher (GO-fur) is the Hebrew word for the kind of wood Noah used to build his boat. Many scholars think

gopher

it was what we call cypress wood today. (Genesis 6:14)

Goshen (GO-shen) was the name of an area in Egypt. This is where the Israelites lived from the time of Joseph to Moses. Goshen was on the east side of the Nile River, near where it flows into the Mediterranean Sea. (Genesis 45:10; 47:6,27)

gospel (GOS-p'l) means "good news." It refers to Jesus' life, death and rising to life again. The first four books of the New Testament are called the gospels because they tell the good news of what Jesus has done for us. (Philippians 1:5,7,12; 2 Thessalonians 1:8) See "Good News."

governor (GUV-er-ner) in the Bible means a person who is in charge of a country or an area. But he worked for a more important ruler. For example, Joseph was governor for the king of Egypt. Also, when the Babylonians took over Judah, they didn't allow the Jews to have their own king. The Babylonians chose a governor to rule that area. (Genesis 42:6; 2 Kings 25:22-25; Matthew 27:2; Acts 23:26)

grace is God's kindness and love shown to us, even though we do not deserve them. Part of God's grace is his forgiveness. He forgives us for the wrong things we do. He even let Jesus take the punishment for our sins. (John 1:14; Acts 15:11; Romans 5:1,2,8; 1 Corinthians 15:10; Ephesians 2:4)

grave is the place where a dead person's body is buried. In Bible lands sometimes a hole was dug in the earth. But often the ground was too rocky; so, the dead were often buried in caves or holes dug in the sides of hills. Abraham bought a cave where he, Sarah, Isaac, Rebekah, Jacob and Leah were all buried. The dead person's body was usually wrapped in cloth. Coffins were not used as they are today, except by the Egyptians. And since Joseph died in Egypt, his body was put in one. (Genesis 23:17-20; 35:19-20; 49:29; 50:13,26; Exodus 13:19; Joshua 24:32; Matthew 27:59-60)

Great Sea See "Mediterranean Sea."

Greece was once the most powerful nation in southeast Europe. In the

New Testament it was called Achaia. Athens, its capital, is still a great city today. The apostle Paul preached in Athens. (Acts 17:16; 20:2)

Greek is the language of the people of Greece. The New Testament was first written in the Greek language. Also, a person from the country of Greece is called a Greek. (John 19:20; Acts 14:1; 16:1,3; 21:37; Colossians 3:11)

H

Habakkuk (ha-BAK-uk) was a prophet who wrote about the same time as Jeremiah, when Babylon was capturing Judah. Habakkuk didn't understand why God would let his people be punished by a nation worse than his own. Habakkuk ends by saying that even when problems come, he will still praise God.

Hades (HAY-deez) is where the dead, both good and bad, are. (Acts 2:27, 31; Revelation 1:18)

Hagar (HAY-gar) was Sarah's slave girl. Her son Ishmael made fun of Isaac, Sarah's son. So Sarah sent Hagar and her son away. They were about to die when an angel rescued them. They were promised that Ishmael would be the beginning of a great nation of people. (Genesis 16; 21)

Haggai (HAG-ay-eye) was a prophet in Jerusalem when the Israelites came back from Babylon. They had started to rebuild the Temple, but they became too concerned about other things and didn't finish. In his book, Haggai encouraged the Israelites to finish the job.

Ham was Noah's youngest son. His descendants became the peoples of southern Arabia, Ethiopia, Egypt and Canaan. (Genesis 6:10; 9:18; 10:6-20)

Haman (HAY-man) was the chief officer under Ahasuerus, king of Persia. He hated a Jew named Mordecai. So, he planned to have all the Jews in Persia killed. But Esther, the queen, was a Jewish woman. She told the king about Haman's plot. As his punishment, Haman was hanged on the gallows he had built to hang Mordecai. (Esther 3–9)

hands, laying on of, is a ceremony where one person places his hands upon another. It was a sign of several different things in the Bible.

Sometimes it was a way of showing that someone was given a special job to do. Moses laid his hands on Joshua to show that he would take Moses' place. Jesus often laid his hands on people when healing them. The apostles laid their hands on people to give them the power of the Holy Spirit. (Deuteronomy 34:9; Mark 5:23; 6:5; Acts 8:17-19)

Hannah (HAN-uh) was the mother of Samuel. She wanted a child very much, but she did not have one for a long time. One day she promised

God that if she had a son, he would serve in the Lord's house. Later, she and her husband Elkanah had a boy named Samuel. When he was old enough, Hannah took him to the Holy Tent to work with Eli the priest. Samuel grew up to be a great leader of God's people. (1 Samuel 1–2)

Word Clues

handwriting on the wall
is a phrase that comes from Daniel 5: 5-6. God made a human hand write a message on the wall of the palace to warn King Belshazzar that his kingdom was coming to an end. Today when we say, "I can see the handwriting on the wall," we mean we know what is about to happen.

Haran (HAY-ran) is a city that is now in the country of Turkey. Abraham lived there after leaving his home in Ur. Later he sent a servant back to Haran to find a wife for Isaac. Jacob also met his wives there. (Genesis 11:31; 12:4; 29:4)

harlot See "prostitute."

harp was the favorite musical instrument of the Jews. Jubal was mentioned as the first one to play the harp. David played a harp to calm Saul when he was upset. The frame of the harp was made of wood. We don't know how many strings harps had in Bible times. It may have been 8, 10 or 12. (Genesis 4:21; 1 Samuel 10:5; 16:23; 2 Samuel 6:5; 1 Kings 10:12)

harvest means gathering crops when they are ripe. For the Israelites there were three harvest times. Barley was ripe in the spring, wheat in the summer and fruit in the fall. The first part of the crop was to be given to the Lord. And some of the crop was to be left in the field for the poor. This gathering of what was left is sometimes called "gleaning." (Leviticus 19:9; 23:10-22; Deuteronomy 24:19-21; Ruth 2) See also "farmer's year" and "gleaning."

heart in the Bible usually means the mind or feelings. It is not talking about the physical heart that pumps blood through the body. (Deuteronomy 30:10-17; Psalm 26:2; Proverbs 15:13-15; Mark 12:30; Luke 2:19; 6:45; 12:34; Acts 2:46)

heaven (HEV-'n) is the home of God. In the New Testament it is said to be a place where there is no pain, no crying, no sadness, no night and no death. Jesus showed us his love by leaving heaven and coming to earth to die on a cross. God's people will live in heaven with him forever. (John 3:13; 6:38-40; Acts 7:56; 2 Corinthians 5:1-10; 1 Peter 1:4; Revelation 21:4)

Hebrews (HEE-brooz) is another name for the Jewish people. The book of Hebrews is a letter written

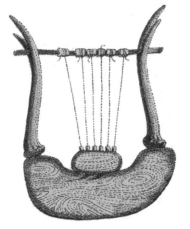

harp

to Jewish Christians. (2 Corinthians 11:22; Philippians 3:5)

Hebron (HEE-bron) is a city about 20 miles southwest of Jerusalem. Abraham and several of his family were buried there. Hebron is where David became king. He ruled from Hebron for seven years before moving to Jerusalem. Later, Absalom made Hebron his capital when he tried to take over the kingdom from David. (Genesis 23:17-20; 2 Samuel 2:1-11; 5:1-13; 15:7-11)

heir (AIR) is the person who is supposed to inherit what belongs to a relative. The heir usually receives these things when the relative dies. Because through Christ we can be adopted children of God, Christians are heirs of God's riches. (Genesis 15:3-4; 2 Samuel 14:7; Galatians 4:1)

hell is the home of the devil. It is the place of punishment forever for those who turn against God. Hell is described in the New Testament as a place of fire, pain, sorrow and sadness. (Matthew 23:33; 25:41; 2 Peter 2:4,9; Revelation 20:14-15; 21:8)

helmet was worn by soldiers to pro-

tect their heads in battle. Some were probably made of leather. But both Goliath and Saul wore bronze helmets. The Bible also says that our salvation protects us from the devil as a helmet protects a soldier. (1 Samuel 17:5,38; 2 Chronicles 26:14; Ephesians 6:17; 1 Thessalonians 5:8)

helping is something we learn from God. Many times the Bible tells us ways that God helps us. He rescues those in trouble. He provides food. He even helps us when we don't know just what to say when we pray. Once Samuel set up a stone and called it "The Stone of Help." This was to remind the Israelites how God had helped them. Because God helps us, we should look for ways to help others. (Genesis 49:25; 1 Samuel 7:12; Psalms 28:7; 121:1-2; Acts 9:36; 16:9; Romans 8:26; Philippians 4:3; Hebrews 6:10)

Herod (HEH-rud) was the name of four different rulers in the New Testament:

Herod I (Herod the Great) was king of the country of Palestine from the year 40 B.C. until about 4 B.C. He tried to kill the baby Jesus because Jesus was called a "king." Herod thought Jesus was an earthly king and would take away his throne. (Matthew 2:1-16; Luke 1:5)

Herod Agrippa I was the king of Palestine for about three years (A.D. 41-44). He was the grandson of Herod I. He had the apostle James killed and the apostle Peter arrested. He did it to please the Jews who hated Jesus' followers. Later, this man was eaten by worms

H

and died because he let the people treat him like a god. (Acts 12:1-21)

Herod Agrippa II was king of Palestine from the year A.D. 52 to 70. He was a great-grandson to Herod I. He heard the apostle Paul speak while visiting Festus. Then Festus sent Paul to Caesar for trial. (Acts 25:13,26; 26:1-32)

Herod Antipas was the son of Herod I. He had John the Baptist's head cut off. Later, Jesus was sent to this man for trial. He ruled from the year 4 B.C. to about A.D. 39. (Matthew 14:1; Mark 6:14; Luke 23:6)

Herodias (heh-ROW-dee-us) was the granddaughter of Herod I. She was the wife of Philip, Herod Antipas' brother. She hated John the Baptist because he told her she was a sinner. So, she had her daughter ask Herod to kill John. Herod had John's head cut off and brought to Herodias' daughter on a platter as she had asked. (Matthew 14:3-12)

Hezekiah (hez-eh-KY-uh) was one of the good kings of Judah. He worked to get rid of idol worship in the land. He had a tunnel cut through rock to bring water into Jerusalem. (2 Kings 18–20; 2 Chronicles 29–32; Isaiah 36–39)

higgaion (hig-GI-on) is probably a musical word. It seems to mean "to meditate." So it may mean a time to think quietly during a song. (Psalm 9:16)

high place is a name sometimes given to a place of worship for false gods. Altars for these idols were often built on top of a hill. The people thought being on a hill made them closer to their god. The Israelites were told to destroy the high places so they would not be tempted to use them. (Numbers 33:52; 1 Kings 14:23; 2 Chronicles 31:1; 33:3)

high priest was the most important religious leader of the Jewish people. He was often as important as the king. Caiaphas was the high priest when Jesus was killed. Annas was another high priest at that time. (Matthew 26:3,57; Acts 23:2-5)

Hilkiah (hil-KY-ah) was the name of several priests in the Old Testament.

Hilkiah was high priest when Josiah was king. He found the scroll of the Law that had been lost in the Temple for many years. He gave the scroll to Shaphan, who read it to King Josiah. They worked to bring the people closer to God. (2 Kings 22–23; 2 Chronicles 34)

Hilkiah, another man, later returned to Jerusalem with Zerubbabel. This was the group that left Babylon to rebuild the Temple. (Nehemiah 12:7)

Hinnom, Valley of, was an area just outside of Jerusalem. It was a dumping ground where trash was burned. False gods had been worshiped there. The Greek name for this place (Gehenna) became the New Testament word for "hell." Because the Valley of Hinnom was such an awful place, no one wanted to go there. (Jeremiah 19:1-13)

Hiram (HY-rum) was the king of Tyre when David and Solomon were kings over Israel. He made friends with both of them. Hiram sent carpenters, stone workers and fine wood builders to help build David's

high priest

house. Solomon asked him for trees and workers when building the Temple, and Hiram helped him then also. Solomon's and Hiram's ships traveled together for several years. Look in 1 Kings 10 to see what things they brought back. (2 Samuel 5:11; 1 Kings 5:1-18; 9:11-27; 10:22)

Hittites (HIT-tites) were people who lived in what is now Turkey. They also lived in the land of Canaan before the Israelites came there. The Hittites may have been the first people to learn about smelting and working with iron. One of David's soldiers was a Hittite named Uriah. (Genesis 23:3-16; Exodus 3:8; Joshua 1:4; 2 Samuel 11:3)

holy (HO-lee) means pure, belonging to and willing to serve God. God's people are called "holy people." (Exodus 3:5; 22:31; 31:13; 1 Corinthians 1:2; Ephesians 1:4; Philemon 4; 1 Peter 1:15-16)

Holy of Holies See "Most Holy Place."

Holy Place This was a room in the Holy Tent and the Temple. The priests came to this room every day to burn incense to the Lord. Each week fresh loaves of bread were placed on the table there. A curtain separated the Holy Place from the Most Holy Place. (Exodus 26:31-35; 31:11; Leviticus 6:30) See "bread that shows we are in God's presence."

Holy Spirit (HO-lee SPIH-rit) is one of the three persons of God. The other two persons are God the Father and God the Son (Jesus). The Holy Spirit helped the apostles do miracles. He led men to write God's word. The Holy Spirit lives in Christians today. He is also called the Spirit of Christ, the Spirit of God, and the Comforter. (Genesis 1:2; John 3:5-8; 16:13; Acts 2:1-4; 5:32; Romans 5:5; 8:9-16; 2 Peter 1:20-21)

Holy Tent See "Meeting Tent."

hope is looking forward to something you really expect to happen. Christians hope to go to heaven to live with God forever. (Psalm 25; Lamentations 3:21-25; Romans 5:3-5; 8:24-25; 15:13; 2 Thessalonians 2:16-17)

Hophni (HOF-nee) and **Phinehas** (FIN-ee-us) were the sons of Eli the priest. They were also priests, but they did not care about the Lord. They stole meat that was supposed to be sacrificed to God. Eli did not like what Hophni and Phinehas were doing, but he did not stop them. So, as punishment, Eli and his sons all died on the same day, and Samuel became the new priest. (1 Samuel 2:12-34; 3:11–4:18)

Horeb, Mount, See "Sinai, Mount."

horses are mentioned many times in the Bible. But they were not usually used for sport or pleasure. Horses were mainly used in war. They pulled

chariots or were ridden by soldiers. So, most horses were owned by kings. (Exodus 14:9,23; Joshua 11:4;

1 Kings 10:26-29; Esther 6:8-11; Psalm 33:17)

hosanna (ho-ZAN-ah) is a Hebrew word that means "save us now." In Jesus' time it was used as a shout of joy in praising God. Hosanna is what the people shouted as Jesus entered Jerusalem. And children shouted it when he was in the Temple. (Psalm 118:25; Matthew 21:9,15)

Hosea (ho-ZEE-uh) was a prophet who lived about 700 years before Christ. He was married to a woman who was not faithful to him. In his book, Hosea showed how the people of Israel were like his wife. She had done wrong, but he still loved her and wanted her back. Israel had also done wrong, but God still loved them and wanted them to come back to him. (Hosea 1–14)

hospitality (HAHS-pih-TAL-i-tee) means being helpful to guests and strangers, especially travelers. In Bible times there were few inns or hotels. And many of them were not good places to stay. So, travelers often stayed in other people's homes. The Bible tells Christians to help each other in this way. The Bible says some people have had angels in their houses without knowing it. (Genesis 18:1-16; 19:1-3; Romans 12:13; 1 Timothy 5:10; Hebrews 13:2; 1 Peter 4:9)

hosts means "armies." In the Old Testament God is sometimes called "The Lord of Hosts." This means "the Lord of heaven's armies." That is what David called God when talking to Goliath. He was letting Goliath know about God's power. (1 Samuel 17:45; 2 Samuel 5:10; 1 Kings 18:15; Psalm 46:7-11; 84:1-12)

houses in Bible times were often one-story buildings. They were made of stones or mud bricks. The roof was usually flat, so people could use it for

drying things such as flax and fruit, as an extra room, a place for worship and a place to sleep in summer. Peter went up on the roof to pray. (Joshua 2; Matthew 7:24-27; Luke 5:18-20; Acts 10:9)

Huldah (HUL-duh) was a woman prophet. When Josiah was king, a scroll of the law was found in the Temple. Josiah sent his chief helpers to ask Hulda about God's words written on the scroll. Hulda said that God would send trouble to the people because of their sin. But because Josiah showed God he was sorry, God promised Josiah that he would die before the trouble came. (2 Kings 22:14-20; 2 Chronicles 34:22)

humble means not bragging or calling attention to yourself. The humble person thinks about other people. (Proverbs 29:23; James 4:6; 1 Peter 5:5)

hymn (HIM) is a song that teaches us about God or praises him. (Ephesians 5:19; Colossians 3:16)

hypocrite (HIP-oh-krit) comes from the word for an actor on a stage. In the Bible it is a person who acts as if he is good but isn't. (Matthew 6:2,5,16; 7:3-5; Luke 13:15-17)

hyssop (HIS-op) is a small bushy plant. Today it is called "marjoram."

It was used like a brush by the Hebrews for sprinkling in their cleansing ceremonies. (Exodus 12:22; Psalm 51:7; John 19:29)

I

Ichabod (ICK-ah-bod) was a grandson of Eli. His name means "Where is the glory?" He was born the day his father and grandfather died.

This was when the Philistines stole Israel's Holy Box. His mother named him Ichabod because she said, "Israel's glory is gone." (1 Samuel 4:21)

Iconium (eye-KOH-nee-um) was a city in Galatia in New Testament times. It is called Konya, Turkey today. When Paul preached there, many Jews became angry and caused trouble. They even followed him to another town and tried to kill him. (Acts 14:1-7, 19-23)

idol (EYE-d'l) is a false god. The non-Jewish people often worshiped statues they made from wood, stone or

metal. They worshiped these idols instead of the true God of heaven. (Leviticus 19:4; 2 Kings 17:12-17; Acts 7:40-43; 17:16-23; 1 Thessalonians 1:9)

immorality (IM-mor-RAL-i-tee) See "sin."

immortality (IM-mor-TAL-i-tee) means life after death. This new life lasts forever and cannot be destroyed. Very little was known about immortality in Old Testament days.

But Jesus died to give us this new life. (Daniel 12:2; Romans 2:6-7; 1 Corinthians 15:54; 2 Timothy 1:10) See also "eternal life."

incense (IN-senz) was a spice burned to make a sweet smell. This was done by the priests in the Meeting Tent and the Temple. A special altar

was used to burn incense as worship to God. Since the smoke seemed to go up to God, this reminded people of prayer. (Exodus 30:1-10, 34-38; Psalm 141:2; Luke 1:9; Revelation 8:3-4)

inheritance (in-HEH-ri-tence) means something valuable that is handed down within the family. Parents or grandparents often leave money or property for their children or grandchildren. In the Old Testament, God told the Israelites that their land in Canaan was like an inheritance from God. In the New Testament eternal life is like an inheritance for Christians. (Deuteronomy 10:9; 19:14; Proverbs 13:22; Romans 8:17; Colossians 1:11-12; 3:23-24)

iniquity See "sin."

inkpot was a container in which writing ink was stored. It had an opening through which the writer could dip the point of a pen into the ink.

inkpot

inn is a place for travelers to spend the night. In Bible times inns were not as nice as motels today. Sometimes they were just a walled-in area with no roof. The people and animals stayed in stalls around the walls. Travelers brought their own food and bedding. (Luke 2:7; 10:34)

inspiration (IN-spi-RAY-shun) means "God-breathed." It is a word we use to show that the Bible writers wrote what God wanted them to write. We don't always know how this happened. Sometimes they saw visions from God. Peter said that the Old Testament prophets were led by the Holy Spirit. This made them able to speak words from God. We know the Bible is true because it was inspired by God. (Psalm 119:142-144; 1 Corinthians 2:12-13; 2 Timothy 3:16; 2 Peter 1:20-21; Revelation 22:18-19)

Isaac (EYE-zak) means "laughter." He was the son of Abraham and Sarah. He was named Isaac because Sarah laughed when she heard the angel tell Abraham she would have a baby. She thought she was too old. God tested Abraham by asking him to offer Isaac as a sacrifice on an altar. When God saw that Abraham would obey him, he saved Isaac's life. (Genesis 21–26; Mark 12:26; Hebrews 11:17-20)

Isaiah (eye-ZAY-uh) was a prophet who lived about 700 years before Christ. He lived in Jerusalem when Judah was in danger from the Assyrians. Isaiah often gave God's message to king Hezekiah. He also wrote the book of Isaiah. He told the people that they would be punished for their sins, but then good times would return. Isaiah said that God would send his son, the Messiah. Chapter 53 especially is about what Jesus would do. (2 Kings 19–20; Isaiah 6; 53)

Ishbosheth (ish-BOW-sheth) was a son of Saul. After Saul and Jonathan died, he was king over part of the Israelites. David was king over the rest. But Ishbosheth was killed by two of his army leaders. So David became king over all Israel. (2 Samuel 2–4)

Ishmael (ISH-may-el) was the son of Abraham and Hagar. Isaac and Ishmael did not get along well with each other. Their mothers did not get along well either. So, Hagar and Ishmael had to leave. God sent an angel to help them in the desert. Ishmael grew up to have great skill with a bow and arrow. His many descendants became the Arabs of the desert. (Genesis 16; 21; 25:7-18; 37:25-28)

Israel (IZ-rah-el) is a Hebrew word that means "he who strives with

God." When Jacob struggled with an angel at Bethel, God named him Israel. The 12 tribes of the Jewish nation were descendants of Jacob. They were called Israelites. (Exodus 3:16-18; Psalm 73:1; Luke 1:68; Acts 2:36; 5:33-36)

Issachar (IS-uh-car) was a son of Jacob and Leah. His descendants were the tribe of Issachar. In the promised land they lived between the southern end of Lake Galilee and Mt. Tabor. (Genesis 30:18; 49:14-15; Numbers 1:28-29; Judges 5:15)

ivory (EYE-voh-ree) comes from elephant tusks. It is creamy white and similar to bone. Ivory is expensive. In Bible times, only rich people had it. Kings used it to make thrones, statues or other decorations and to cover walls. (1 Kings 10:18; 22:39; 2 Chronicles 9:17; Psalm 45:8; Amos 3:15; 6:4)

ivory

Jabbok River (JAB-ok) is a stream about fifty miles long. It runs into the Jordan River near the Dead Sea. Jacob was beside the Jabbok River when he had his unusual meeting with God. Read the story to find out what happened. (Genesis 32:22-32)

Jabesh-Gilead (JAY-besh GIL-ee-ad) was a small town on the east side of the Jordan River. Once the Ammonites were threatening to be very cruel to the men of Jabesh-Gilead. Saul had just been made king. When he heard about their danger, he got his soldiers together quickly and rescued Jabesh-Gilead. The men of Jabesh-Gilead did not forget it. When Saul died, they risked their lives to get his body and bury it. (1 Samuel 11:1-14; 31:8-13)

Jabin (JAY-bin) was the name of two Canaanite kings of Hazor.

Jabin led a group of kings against Israel when they first came to the promised land. But Joshua defeated them. (Joshua 11:1-11)

Another Jabin captured Israel. He was very cruel to them. But

Deborah and Barak brought the people together and defeated Jabin. (Judges 4–5)

jackal (JAK-ul) is a small animal similar to a fox. Jackals travel in

packs (groups). They hunt for food at night. The foxes in the story of Samson were probably jackals. (Judges 15:4)

Jacob (JAY-cub) was 1 of the sons of Isaac. Jacob had 12 sons, and each son was the head of a tribe. The 12 tribes were God's chosen people. (Genesis 25–36; Matthew 1:2; 8:11; John 4:6)

Jacob's Portion (JAY-cubs POR-shun) is a name for God. It means that God cares for Jacob's people, the Israelites. (Jeremiah 10:16; 51:19)

Jacob's Well (JAY-cubs) was the place where Jesus talked with a Samaritan woman. It was near the town of Sychar in Samaria. Jacob's well is still there today. (Genesis 33:19; John 4)

Jairus (jay-EYE-rus) was a ruler of the synagogue. He travelled to find Jesus to make his sick daughter well, but she died while Jairus was gone. Jesus went with Jairus to the house anyway. Then Jesus raised her back to life. (Matthew 9:18-26; Mark 5:21-43; Luke 8:40-56)

James was the name of several men in the New Testament:

James, the brother of Jesus, was a respected leader in the church in Jerusalem. He probably wrote the book of James in the New Testament. (Matthew 13:55; John 7:5; Acts 12:17; 21:18; Galatians 1:19)

James, the son of Alphaeus, was one of Jesus' apostles. He may have been a cousin to Jesus. (Matthew 10:3)

James, the son of Zebedee, was an apostle of Jesus and a brother of the apostle John. He was killed by Herod Agrippa I. (Matthew 10:2; Mark 10:35,41; Acts 12:2)

James, letter of, was written by James, who was probably the brother of Jesus. It is filled with helpful instructions about how we should live. James writes about such things as being tempted to do wrong, listening and obeying. Chapter three tells how important it is to control what we say. Read James 5:16 to see what happens when a good person prays.

Japheth (JAY-fith) was one of Noah's three sons. His descendants became the people who lived north and west of the Hebrews. (Genesis 5:32; 6:10; 7:13; 9:18-19; 10:1-5)

Jashar, book of, is a book mentioned in the Bible. But it is not part of the Bible. The book of Jashar must have been a book of poems and songs that was well known to the Israelites. The book is now lost. (Joshua 10:12-13; 2 Samuel 1:17-27)

Jason (JAY-son) was a Christian in the city of Thessalonica. When Paul was in town he stayed at Jason's house. (Acts 17:5-9)

J

javelin (JAV-eh-lin) is a long-handled weapon with a sharp point on one

end. It is very much like a spear. (1 Samuel 17:45)

jealous (JEH-lus) can mean two very different things. The good kind of jealousy is a strong feeling for someone. The Bible says that God is jealous. It means he loves us and does not want us to love the wrong gods. The bad kind of jealousy means disliking someone who has something you want for yourself. Joseph's brothers were jealous of him and the special coat his father gave him. (Genesis 37:11; Exodus 34:14; Deuteronomy 6:15; Galatians 5:19-20; James 3:14-16)

Jebusites (JEB-you-sites) were the people who lived around Jerusalem before the time of David. They called their city Jebus. David captured Jebus and changed its name to Jerusalem. (Joshua 15:63; Judges 19:10-11; 1 Chronicles 11:4-9)

Jehoahaz (jeh-HO-uh-haz) was the name of two kings.

Jehoahaz, the son of Jehu, was king of Israel. He worshiped idols. So, God allowed him to be defeated by Syria. He lived about 800 years before Christ. (2 Kings 13:1-9)

Jehoahaz, the son of Josiah, was king of Judah for only three months. He was captured by the king of Egypt and taken to Egypt as a prisoner. (2 Kings 23:31-34)

Jehoash, the son of Jehoahaz, was a king of Israel. He lived about 800 years before Christ. He was also called Joash. (2 Kings 13–14)

Jehoiachin (jeh-HO-uh-kin) was the next-to-last king of Judah. He ruled for only three months in 597 B.C. Then Nebuchadnezzar took him as a prisoner to Babylon. Later, he was released and lived in the Babylonian court. (2 Kings 24:8-17; 25:27-30; 2 Chronicles 36:9-10; Jeremiah 52:31-34)

Jehoiada (jeh-HO-yah-duh) was the chief priest in Jerusalem. This was during the rules of Ahaziah, Athaliah and Joash. He helped get rid of the evil queen, Athaliah. Joash was next in line to be king, but he was only seven years old. Jehoiada made Joash king, but he ruled for the boy until Joash was old enough to rule for himself. (2 Kings 11–12; 2 Chronicles 23–24)

Jehoiakim (jeh-HO-uh-kim) was king of Judah about 600 B.C. He was the son of Josiah. But Jehoiakim undid the good things his father had done. He did not listen to the prophet Jeremiah. Jeremiah warned him not to fight against Babylon, but he fought them anyway and was killed. (2 Kings 23:34–24:6;

24:6; 1 Chronicles 3:15-16; Jeremiah 26:1-23; 36:1-23)

Jehoram (jeh-HOR-am) (or Joram) was the fifth king of Judah. He was married to Athaliah who was evil like her mother Jezebel. Jehoram killed his own brothers so none of them would try to be king. He also led the people to worship false gods. The prophet Elijah wrote him a letter that said he would be punished for his terrible sins. Read the letter and see what his punishment was. (2 Chronicles 21:4-20)

Jehoshaphat (jeh-HOSH-uh-fat) was one of the good kings of Judah. He got rid of the places for worshiping false gods. So "the Lord made Jehoshaphat a strong king." He improved the army and built strong, walled cities to protect the country. (2 Chronicles 17–20)

Jehovah (jeh-HOVE-uh) is a word used in some Bibles for the name of God. Now most Bibles use "the Lord" for that name instead.

Jehu (JEE-hew) was at first an army captain under King Joram. But God chose Jehu to take Joram's place as king of Israel. Elisha the prophet appointed Jehu king for God and told him to destroy Jordan. So, he had Joram and his evil relatives killed. Jehu did stop the worship of the false god, Baal. But he still allowed the worship of golden calves. (2 Kings 9–10)

Jephthah (JEF-thuh) was one of the judges of Israel. Before going into a battle, he promised to sacrifice the first thing that came to meet him when he got home if the Israelites won. They did win, but when he got home his daughter was first to come out to meet him. He did as he had promised. This sacrifice of his daughter may mean that he gave her to serve God and not get married. (Judges 11:1–12:7)

Jeremiah (jer-eh-MY-ah) was a prophet who warned the people of Judah. He told them they were disobeying God and would be punished. He had a very difficult life, but he stayed faithful to God. He lived to see Jerusalem destroyed and the people taken to Babylon. (2 Chronicles 35:25; 36:21-22; Jeremiah 1–2; 20:1-6; 28:5; 36–40)

Jericho (JEHR-ih-ko) is the oldest city in the world. God caused the walls of Jericho to fall down when the Israelites did what God told them. This was their first victory in the promised land. Jericho was rebuilt and destroyed several times. In

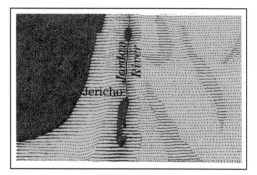

New Testament times Herod rebuilt it a mile away from where it had been. Here Jesus healed blind Bartimaeus and met Zacchaeus. Jericho is called "the city of palm trees" because a spring there makes it an oasis in the desert. (Joshua 2; 6; 1 Kings 16:34; Nehemiah 3:2; Mark 10:46-52; Luke 19:1-10)

Jeroboam (jeh-ro-BO-am) was the name of two kings of Israel.

Jeroboam, the son of Jehoash, was king of Israel about 150 years after the first Jeroboam. He won several victories over Israel's neighbors. But he was guilty of the same sins as the first Jeroboam. The prophet Amos warned him to turn the people toward God, but he did not listen. (2 Kings 14:23-29; Amos 7:7-17)

Jeroboam, the son of Nebat, was the first ruler of the northern kingdom of Israel. He turned against Rehoboam who was Solomon's son. He made golden calves for the people to worship. Future kings of Israel followed his bad example. (1 Kings 11:26–14:20)

Jerusalem (jeh-ROO-suh-lem) is sometimes called "Zion" or the "City of David." It was the greatest city of the country of Palestine. It was the center of the Jewish religion because the Temple was there. Jesus was killed on a cross near Jerusalem. The city was destroyed by the Roman army in the year A.D. 70. Later, it was rebuilt in the same place by the Moslems and is a great city today in the Middle East. (2 Samuel 5:5-6; 2 Chronicles 36:14,19; Ezra 1:1-11; Luke 2:22-45; 13:34; 24:13,18,33,47,49; Acts 2:5,14) See "Zion."

Jesse (JEH-see) was the father of King David. He had many sons, but the Bible only gives the names of a few. (1 Samuel 16–17; 1 Chronicles 2:13-15)

Jesus (JEE-zus) means "savior." He is the Son of God. He was born to Mary, a young Jewish woman. Mary was told by the angel Gabriel that she would have a baby boy. She was to name him "Jesus" because he would save his people from their sins. He is also called "Christ" and "Messiah." He lived a perfect life and never sinned. But he was killed on a cross by Roman soldiers near Jerusalem. Then, he came back to life and now lives in heaven with his Father, God. He is one of the three persons of God. The other two persons are God the Father, and God the Holy Spirit. (Matthew 1:21; Luke 2:21; 3:23; John 20:19; Acts 1:19, 36; 4:10; Philippians 2:10-11) See "Christ" and "Messiah."

Jesus was a common name among Jewish people, so there were other less important men in the New Testament named Jesus, too. (Colossians 4:11)

Jethro (JETH-row), sometimes called Reuel, was the father of Moses' wife. Moses lived with him and cared for his sheep for forty years. He gave Moses some good suggestions on how to handle the Israelites in the wilderness. (Exodus 2:16-18; 3:1; 18:1-27)

Jew (JOO) at first meant someone from the tribe of Judah. Judah was 1 of Jacob's 12 sons and the head of 1 of the 12 tribes of Israel. Later, the word Jew meant any person in any of the 12 tribes (Hebrews 1–13). A person who is a not a Jew is called a Gentile or non-Jew. Jesus was a Jew. (Ezra 4:12; Matthew 2:2; 28:11-15; Acts 2:5; Romans 1:16; 10:12)

Jezebel (JEZ-eh-bell) was the evil wife of King Ahab. She worshiped the false gods Baal and Asherah. Many Israelites followed her example and worshiped the false gods, too. Jezebel had many prophets of God killed. She even had a man named Naboth killed so Ahab could have his vineyard. Jezebel died a violent death because of her sins. (1 Kings 16:31-33; 18:4,19; 19:1-2; 21:1-24; 2 Kings 9:30-38)

Jezreel (JEZ-reel) was the name of a town and a valley near the Jordan River and Mount Gilboa. The valley separated Galilee from Samaria. Naboth's vineyard was there. (1 Samuel 29:1,11; 1 Kings 4:12; 21:1-16; 2 Kings 9:30-37)

Joab (JO-ab) was the commander of King David's army. He was a good fighter, but he was also cruel. He killed Abner who was trying to make peace. And he was told not to kill Absalom but did it anyway. Joab was killed for trying to keep Solomon from becoming king. (2 Samuel 2–3; 10–11; 14; 18–20; 24; 1 Kings 1–2)

Joanna (jo-ANN-uh) was a woman Jesus healed. Then she used her money to help Jesus and the apostles. She was one of the women who prepared Jesus' body to be buried. Joanna was also one of those who saw that Jesus had been raised from death. (Luke 8:2-3; 23:55–24:11)

Joash (JO-ash) was the name of three people in the Old Testament:

Joash, Gideon's father. Read to see how he protected his son when people were angry with him. (Judges 6:28-32)

Joash, the son of Ahaziah, was a king of Judah. He became king when he was only seven years old.

Jehoiada helped him rule until Joash was older. He was also called Jehoash. (2 Kings 11–12)

Joash, son of Jehoahaz, was a king of Israel. He lived about 800 years before Christ. He, too, was called Jehoash. (2 Kings 13–14)

Job (JOBE) is the main character in the book of Job. He was a very good man. Job lost his money, health and family. His wife told him to curse God for allowing this to happen. But he didn't. Then Job's friends tried to tell him that his troubles were punishment for his sins. But he was sure that wasn't true. Job didn't understand why it had happened, and he was very upset. But he still trusted God. Finally, God spoke and told Job that there are some things man cannot understand. In the end Job was given back more than he had lost. (Job 1–42)

Joel (JO-el) was a prophet who wrote the book of Joel. He talked about Judah's crops being destroyed because of locusts and no rain. He warned God's people to start obeying him. Joel also told of God's promise to send the Holy Spirit. (Joel 1–3; Acts 2:17-21)

Johanan (jo-HAY-nan) was a Jewish army captain. He stayed in Judah after Nebuchadnezzar had taken away many of the Jews as captives to Babylon. Johanan warned Gedaliah (the governor of Jerusalem) that someone was trying to kill him. But Gedaliah didn't believe Johanan, and Gedaliah was murdered. Later, Johanan led many Jews to escape to Egypt. The prophet Jeremiah warned them not to go, but they would not

J

listen. Johanan even made Jeremiah go with them. (Jeremiah 40–43)

John was the name of several men in the New Testament:

John, the apostle, was one of the sons of Zebedee. He and his brother James were fishermen. He wrote the gospel of John, the books of 1, 2 and 3 John and the book of Revelation. He is sometimes referred to as "the one Jesus loved." John, Peter and James were Jesus' closest friends. (Mark 1:19-20; 9:2; 14:33-34; Acts 3:1-11; Revelation 1:1-4,9)

John the Baptist was Jesus' relative and the son of Elizabeth and Zechariah the priest. He lived in the desert and ate locusts and wild honey. He preached that the Savior, Jesus, was coming soon. Jesus came to John the Baptist to be baptized in the Jordan River. Herod Antipas had John killed by cutting off his head. (Matthew 3:1-17; 11: 11-13; 14:3-12; Luke 1:13-17)

John Mark See Mark.

John, Gospel of, is one of the four books in the New Testament that tells the Good News about Jesus. It was probably the last one written, about A.D. 90. This book was written by John the apostle. It tells us that Jesus was with God before the world began. John tells us about several miracles that the other three gospel writers don't mention. Read John 20:30-31 to find out why John wrote the book.

John, letters of, are three short letters in the New Testament. They were written by John the apostle. In 1 John he reminds us that Jesus was a real man, not just a spirit. The letter also tells us to obey God and ask for forgiveness when we sin. All three letters warn Christians not to listen to people who do not tell the truth about Jesus.

Jonah (JO-nah) was a prophet whom God told to go to the city of Nineveh to preach. Jonah did not want to go; so, he got on a ship sailing the opposite way. But he was swallowed by

a big fish that God had sent. After three days, the fish spat Jonah out on the land. Then he finally obeyed God and went to Nineveh. But he became angry when God forgave the people. The book of Jonah teaches us that God cares about all people and so should we. (Jonah 1–4)

Jonathan (JAH-nah-than) was the oldest son of King Saul. He became a good friend of David. Jonathan was brave and fought well in battles. He and his father were killed together in battle by the Philistines. David wrote a sad song when he heard about it. (1 Samuel 13–14; 18–20; 31:1-6; 2 Samuel 1)

Joppa (JOP-uh) is a Hebrew word

that means "beautiful." In Joppa, Peter brought Tabitha (Dorcas) back to life. There he also had a vision from God of a sheet filled with animals. This vision was teaching him to preach to the non-Jewish people, not just the Jews. Joppa is now a part of the city of Tel Aviv. (Acts 9:36-42; 10:9-36)

Joram, the son of Ahab, was a king of Israel for 12 years. (2 Kings 1:17; 3:1-3)

Jordan (JOR-d'n) is the only large river in the country of Palestine. It runs about 75 miles from Mount

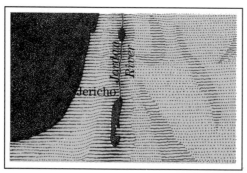

Hermon to the Dead Sea. It also makes two lakes—Lake Huleh and Lake Galilee. Jesus was baptized in the Jordan River near the city of Jericho. (Joshua 3:11-17; 2 Kings 5:10,14; Matthew 3:5-17)

Joseph (JOZ-uf) was the name of several men in the Bible:

Joseph of Arimathea took the body of Jesus down from the cross and buried it in a tomb he had dug for himself. He was a member of the Jewish religious court called the Sanhedrin. (Matthew 27:57-60; Mark 15:43-46)

Joseph of Nazareth was the husband of Mary, Jesus' mother. He

was a carpenter. He may have died when Jesus was a young man because he is not mentioned after Jesus' childhood. The New Testament says he was "a good man." (Matthew 1:18-24; 2:13-23)

Joseph the son of Jacob was 1 of the 12 sons of Israel. His 2 sons, Ephraim and Manasseh, each started a tribe. (Genesis 37–50; Exodus 1:5-8; 13:19; Acts 7:10-14)

Joshua (JAH-shoo-ah) led the Israelites into the promised land. He had been Moses' helper during the years in the wilderness. Moses chose Joshua to take his place. Joshua led the army in battles and divided the land between the tribes. At the end of his life, he challenged the Israelites to decide whom they would serve—God or idols. (Exodus 24:13; Numbers 13; 27:18-23; Deuteronomy 34:9-10; Joshua 1–13; 24)

Joshua, book of, is the sixth book in the Bible. It is the first of the books of history. It tells how Joshua led the Israelites into the promised land. The book ends with the death of Joshua.

Josiah (jo-SY-uh) was king of Judah about 640–609 B.C. He was one of the good kings of the Old Testament. The book of God's Law was found when Josiah was king. So, he destroyed many idols and helped the people obey God in a better way. Josiah was killed in a battle against Egypt. (2 Kings 22–23)

Jotham (JO-tham) was the name of two men in the Old Testament:

Jotham, the son of Gideon, told the first parable in the Bible. It was a story about which tree should be the king of the other trees. The story was to show people that Abimelech was not the man who should be their leader. (Judges 9:1-21, 57)

Jotham, son of Uzziah, was a king of Judah. He was one of the kings who obeyed God. He defeated enemies and made the cities stronger. (2 Kings 15:32-38; 2 Chronicles 27:1-6)

joy is the happy feeling of being right with God and other people. The Bible says that seeing God do great things causes joy in those who love him. The birth of Jesus as savior of the world brought joy to people. Early Christians showed that they could have joy even when they were having problems because they knew they were doing what was right. When the Holy Spirit lives in us, we have joy. (Psalms 16:11; 105:43; Luke 2:10; Acts 13:50-52; Romans 15:13; Galatians 5:22; 1 Peter 1:8; Jude 24)

Jubilee (JOO-bih-lee) was a Jewish celebration that only took place once every 50 years. Israelites were to do three things: (1) give the soil a rest and not farm, (2) free Israelite slaves and (3) return land and houses to their first owners or their children. (Leviticus 25)

Judah (JOO-duh) was the fourth son of Jacob. The descendants of Judah formed the tribe of Judah. Their land was between the Dead Sea and the Mediterranean Sea. Hebron was their most important city. David and his family were from this tribe. (Genesis 29:35; Judges 1:1-19; 2 Samuel 2:4; Matthew 1:2-3; Luke 3:33; Revelation 5:5)

Judah, kingdom of, is the name given to the southern kingdom of Israel. Under kings Saul, David and Solomon, the Israelites were all one nation. But Solomon's son Rehoboam was not a wise king. So, the nation split into two kingdoms. The ten northern tribes were called Israel. The tribes in the south (Judah and Benjamin) started a separate kingdom called Judah. This kingdom lasted from about 930 to 587 B.C. when the Babylonians captured Jerusalem. (1 Kings 12:1-20; 14:21–15:8; 2 Kings 24:18–25:22)

Judas Iscariot (JOO-dus is-CARE-ee-ut) was the apostle who turned against Jesus and handed him over to the Roman soldiers to be killed. For this he was paid only 30 pieces of silver, the price of a slave. Later, Judas killed himself. (Matthew 26:47-50; 27:3-5; John 13:26-30)

Jude (JOOD) was possibly a brother of Jesus and James. In Jesus' early ministry, Jude did not believe Jesus was the Son of God. Later, he believed and became a leader in Christ's church. He wrote the book of Jude in the New Testament. (John 7:5; Jude)

Judea (joo-DEE-uh) was the land of the Jews. It was a district in the country of Palestine. Both Jerusalem and Bethlehem were cities in Judea. John the Baptist began his preaching in the desert of Judea. (Matthew 2:1; Luke 1:5; 2:4; Acts 1:8)

judges (JUHG-es) were the leaders of Israel before Israel had kings. A judge decided who was guilty in court, led the army in battle and was in charge of the government, like a governor. Israel had 15 judges in all. (Judges 2:16-19; 1 Samuel 7:15-17)

Judges, book of, tells the story of the Israelites during the years they were ruled by judges. This was from the time of Joshua until the time of Samuel, the last judge. The same things happened over and over. (1)The Israelites sinned. (2)Their enemies attacked. (3)The Israelites asked God for help. (4)God sent a judge to rescue them. (5)Things went well for a while. (6)They started sinning again.

Judgment Day (JUJ-ment) is the day Christ will judge all people. He will take his followers to live with him forever in heaven. Those who have followed the devil will be sent to live with him in hell forever. (Matthew 11:20-24; Hebrews 9:27-28; 2 Peter 2:9-10; 3:7)

Julius (JOOL-yus) was a Roman soldier. He was in charge of Paul while Paul was being taken to Rome. Julius was kind to Paul and let him visit friends. (Acts 27)

justify (JUS-teh-fy) means to make someone right with God. Sin separates us from God. Since all people sin, all need to be made right with God. No one can do enough good things to make up for his or her sins. So, we need someone without sin to take care of our sin. Jesus did that by dying on the cross for us. If we believe and obey God, he can make us right with him. That is being justified. (Romans 3:20-26; 4:20-25; 5:12-21; Galatians 2:15-16)

K

Kadesh and **Kadesh-Barnea** (KAY-desh BAR-nee-uh) are names of a town in the wilderness. It was an oasis on the way from Egypt to the promised land. The twelve spies were sent out from here to Canaan. Moses' sister Miriam died at Kadesh. And it was at this spot that Moses found out he would not be going into the promised land. (Numbers 13–14; 20:1-11; Deuteronomy 1:19-25; Joshua 10:41; 14:6-8)

Kedar (KEE-dar) was a son of Ishmael. His descendants were known for their beautiful black tents. They were desert nomads. That means they were always traveling with their sheep. They moved from one feeding place to another. (Genesis 25:13; Isaiah 42:11; 60:7)

Kenites (KEE-nites) were a tribe of early metal workers. They lived in Canaan when Abraham moved there. Some of them also lived in

Midian. Moses' wife was a Kenite. Later, both Saul and David made friends with the Kenites. (Genesis 15:19; Judges 1:16; 4:11; 1 Samuel 15:6; 27:10; 30:29)

Keturah (keh-TOO-ruh) was Abraham's second wife. They had six sons. These men became the fathers of many Arab peoples. (Genesis 25: 1-4; 1 Chronicles 1:32-33)

Kidron Valley (KEH-dron) is between Jerusalem and the Mount of Olives. The Gihon Spring is on the west side of the valley. The water from this spring goes into Jerusalem through the Siloam tunnel. The good kings of Judah destroyed idols in the Kidron Valley. Jesus and his followers crossed it going to the Garden of Gethsemane. (2 Samuel 15: 23; 1 Kings 15:13; 2 Kings 23:4; 2 Chronicles 29:16; Mark 14:26; John 18:1)

king was a man who ruled over a city or a nation. A king was not usually chosen by the people. A man often became king because his father was king before him. The Israelites had judges, not kings, for many years. But they wanted to be like the other people around them and have a king. They had three kings before they split into two nations. Then each nation had its own king. In New Testament times kings (like the Herods) were chosen by the Romans. They were allowed to help rule an area. (1 Samuel 8; Matthew 2:1; 1 Peter 2:13-17)

kingdom (KING-d'm) The kingdom of heaven (or kingdom of God) is God ruling in the lives of his people. (Matthew 3:2; 6:33; Luke 9:27; 17: 20-21; John 3:3-5; Hebrews 12:28)

Kings, First and Second, are two Old Testament books that tell of the kings of Israel and Judah for about 400 years. This period of time was from King David's death in 965 B.C. until Jerusalem was destroyed in 587 B.C. The books of Kings were actually one book at first. It was divided into two books about 200 B.C. when the Old Testament was first translated into the Greek language.

King's Highway or **King's Road** is the name for a very old road. It ran from the Gulf of Aqabah (on the Red Sea) all the way to Damascus. There were several strong, walled cities built along it. Moses and the Israelites wanted to travel on the King's Road on their way to the promised land. But the Edomites and Ammonites would not allow them to come through their countries on it. (Numbers 20:17-21; 21:22)

kinnor (KEH-nor) was a musical instrument in Bible times. It was very

much like a small harp. The instrument that David played for King

Saul was probably a kinnor. (1 Samuel 16:23)

Kiriath-Jearim (KEER-yath JEE-ah-rim) was a town in the hills about 12 miles west of Jerusalem. When the Israelites got the Holy Box from the Philistines, they kept it at Kiriath-Jearim for 20 years. (Joshua 9; 1 Samuel 6:20–7:2; 2 Samuel 6:1-15; Nehemiah 7:29; Jeremiah 26:20)

Kishon (KY-shon) is the name of a valley and stream. The stream flows into the Mediterranean Sea near Mount Carmel. The stream was very deep when Sisera and Barak fought there. This was also where Elijah defeated the prophets of Baal. (Judges 4:13; 5:21; 1 Kings 18:40)

kiss in Bible times could show friendship, love or respect. Early Christians kissed each other on the cheek as a greeting. Guests were kissed when they entered someone's house. (Genesis 29:11; Ruth 1:9; 1 Samuel 20:41; Luke 7:38,45; Acts 20:37; Romans 16:16; 1 Peter 5:14)

Kittim (KEH-tim) is the Old Testament name for the island of Cyprus. This is an island in the Mediterranean Sea. (Numbers 24:24; Isaiah 23:1,12)

kneel (NEEL) means to get down on your knees. This was done as a sign

of respect to kings. People often prayed in this position to show respect for God. This was also called "bowing the knees." (1 Kings 8:54; Psalm 95:6; Daniel 6:10; Romans 14:11; Ephesians 3:14; Philippians 2:10)

knowledge, tree of, is a tree in the middle of the garden of Eden. Adam and Eve were told by God not to eat the fruit from this tree even though they could eat from all other trees. Once they ate from it, they knew about evil, which brought sin into the world. (Genesis 2:9,17; 3:1-19)

Kohath (KO-hath) was a son of Levi. He was also the grandfather of Moses, Aaron and Miriam. (Exodus 6:16-20; Numbers 3:17-19)

Kohathites (KO-hath-ites) were the descendants of Kohath. They were one of the three family groups in the tribe of Levi. Their job was to take care of the Holy Box and other furniture in the Most Holy Place. (Numbers 3:27-31; 4:1-20; 1 Chronicles 9:32; 2 Chronicles 20:19)

K

Korah (KO-ruh) was the name of several people in the Old Testament. Here are two of them:

Korah had descendants who were musicians in the Temple. They wrote, and probably sang, several of the psalms. (Psalms 42; 44–49; 84)

Korah, son of Izhar, (perhaps the same one as above) led a group who didn't think Moses should be the leader. Korah and his group were punished. The earth opened and swallowed them to show that God had chosen Moses to be the leader. (Numbers 16)

L

Laban (LAY-ban) was the father of Leah and Rachel. Jacob worked for Laban seven years in order to marry Rachel. But Laban tricked Jacob into marrying Leah, the oldest daughter, instead. So, Jacob had to work seven more years for Rachel, the one he loved. For many years after that, the two men did not get along. See Genesis 31:43-53 to find out how they made peace and what they did to remember it. (Genesis 29–31)

Lachish (LAY-kish) was a city about 30 miles southwest of Jerusalem. Joshua's army defeated Lachish while capturing the land of Canaan. Many years later, Rehoboam rebuilt it and made it into a strong, walled city. It had thick walls, strong towers and a good well. Lachish lasted hundreds of years until the Babylonians destroyed it. (Joshua 10; 2 Kings 14:19; 18:14-21; 2 Chronicles 11:5-12; Nehemiah 11:30)

lamb (LAM) is an animal that the Jews often offered as a sacrifice (gift) to God. Since Jesus died as a sacrifice for us, he is called the Lamb of God that takes away the sins of the world. (Genesis 4:4; 22:7; Exodus 12:3-13; John 1:29,36; 1 Corinthians 5:7)

Lamech (LAY-mek) was the name of two men in the Old Testament.
Lamech was a descendant of Cain. He bragged about killing a man for hitting him. Lamech wrote a song to his wives about the murder. (Genesis 4:18-24)

Lamech, son of Methuselah, was the father of Noah. (Genesis 5: 28-29)

Lamentations (LAM-en-TAY-shunz) means "sadness." It is the name of a book in the Old Testament. The book contains five sad poems or songs. The writer was probably the prophet Jeremiah. He describes how sad the people of Jerusalem were when the Babylonians destroyed the city and took many people captive. But Lamentations is not all sadness. In chapter three there is hope for the future. He writes, "But I have hope when I think of this: The Lord's love never ends. His mercies never stop. They are new every morning." (Lamentations 3:21-23)

lamp in Bible times looked like a small bowl. Inside was olive oil. The bowl was narrower on one end to hold up the wick. Sometimes there was no opening in the lamp, except

a spout on one end where the wick was. Psalm 119 says the Bible is like a lamp. Both the lamp and the Bible let us see what to do and where to go. (Psalm 119:105; Proverbs 6:23; Matthew 25:1-8)

lampstand was a holder to hold a lamp up higher so the light would shine over a larger area. The Holy Tent and the Temple had a gold lampstand. It held seven lamps. (Exodus 25:31-40; 26:35; 1 Kings 7:49)

languages of the Bible were Hebrew, Aramaic and Greek. Most of the Old Testament was written in Hebrew, which was the language the Israelites spoke. But after being captured and taken to Babylon, they also learned Aramaic. So, part of the books of Daniel and Ezra were written in Aramaic. This became the language spoken by most Jews in Israel when Jesus lived. But people also spoke Greek all over that part of the world. So, Greek was the best language for the writing of the New Testament.

Laodicea (lay-ah-deh-SEE-uh) was a town in what is called Turkey today. It was an important town where the people had more money than in other areas. The church there began in Paul's day. But by the time John wrote the book of Revelation, they were more concerned with making money than serving God. (Colossians 2:1; 4:13-16; Revelation 3:14-22)

last supper is the meal Jesus ate with his followers the night before his death. It was the Passover meal that Jews celebrated every year. (Matthew 26:17-30; Mark 14:12-26; Luke 22:7-20; 1 Corinthians 11:23-26)

Latin (LAT-in) was the language spoken by the Roman people during New Testament times. Government workers and soldiers from Rome who were in Israel knew Latin. The sign on the cross above Jesus' head which read "King of the Jews" was written in Latin, Greek and Hebrew. (John 19:20)

laver (LAY-vur) is a name sometimes used for a bowl for washing. The Holy Tent and Temple had a bronze laver. The priests washed their hands

and feet in the bowl to be clean before entering the tent. (Exodus 30:17-19; 1 Kings 7:38)

Law in the Bible usually means the rules God gave his people in the Old Testament. These rules told how people should live together. God also gave detailed instructions about how they were to serve him. The New Testament says that the Law was good, but no one could obey it all, except Jesus. So, now we have a new and better way of serving him through faith by God's grace. (Romans 7:12-13; Galatians 3:19-25; Hebrews 9:15; 10:1-10)

laying on of hands See "hands, laying on of."

L

Lazarus (LAZ-uh-rus) was the name of two men in the New Testament:

Lazarus of Bethany was a brother to Mary and Martha. He was also a very dear friend of Jesus. When he died, Jesus brought him back to life. (John 11:1-45; 12:1-11)

Lazarus, the beggar, was the name of a person in a story Jesus told his followers. (Luke 16:19-31)

Leah (LEE-uh) was a wife of Jacob. He was tricked into marrying her by Laban, her father. She was the mother of 6 sons—Reuben, Simeon, Levi, Judah, Issachar and Zebulun—who were the fathers of 6 of the 12 tribes of Israel. (Genesis 29:15-35; 30:17-21; 35:23; 49:31)

leather (LEH-thur) is made from animal skins, especially sheep and goats. In Bible times leather was used for clothing, belts, shoes, tents

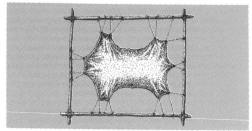

and water containers. Also, strips of leather were sewn together to make a scroll. The books of the Bible were written on scrolls. (Exodus 26:14; 1 Samuel 1:24; 2 Kings 1:8; Ezekiel 16:10; Matthew 3:4)

leaven See "yeast."

Lebanon (LEH-beh-nun) means "white." It is the name of a country north of Israel. In Bible times it was known for its beautiful cedar trees. Its name is taken from the mountains which were often "white" be-

cause they were snow covered. The lower land of Lebanon grew many kinds of fruits and vegetables. The cities of Tyre and Sidon are in Lebanon. Solomon got trees from Lebanon to build the Temple and his palace. (1 Kings 5:1-11; Ezra 3:7; Psalm 92:12; Isaiah 2:13; 14:8)

legion (LEE-jun) was a group of about 6,000 soldiers in the Roman army. There was also a man who told Jesus his name was "Legion." He said that because he had many evil spirits inside him. Jesus made the evil spirits leave the man and go into a herd of pigs nearby. The pigs ran into the sea and drowned. (Mark 5:9; Luke 8:30)

leprosy (LEH-prah-see) is a name for some bad skin diseases. A person with leprosy was called a leper and had to live outside the city. When other people came by, the lepers had to warn them by crying out, "Unclean! Unclean!" (Leviticus 13:45-46; 2 Kings 5:1-27; 2 Chronicles 26:19-23; Matthew 8:3; Luke 17:11-19)

Leviathan (lee-VI-ah-than) was the name for a sea monster. Some people

think it was a crocodile or a dragon. (Job 3:8; 41:1; Psalm 74:14; Isaiah 27:1)

Levites (LEE-vites) were descendants of Levi, one of Jacob's sons.

The priests all came from this tribe. But not all Levites were priests. Those who were not priests worked in the Meeting Tent or Temple in other ways. (Exodus 32:25-29; Numbers 1:47-53; 8:5-26; Deuteronomy 10:8-9; 18:1-8; 1 Kings 12:31; Luke 10:32)

Leviticus (leh-VIT-eh-cus) is the third book in the Bible. It tells about the duties of the Levites who were Israelite priests. It also has many rules about how the Jews were supposed to eat, dress and do business.

lid on the Holy Box is also called the mercy seat. This was the beautiful gold lid on the Box of the Agreement. It had a gold creature with wings on each end of it. This Holy Box was kept in the Most Holy Place of the Meeting Tent and later in the Temple. (Exodus 25:17-22; 26:34; Leviticus 12:2,14-16; Hebrews 9:5)

life, book of, is what the Bible calls the list of those who are God's people. Only those whose names are in the book of life will go to heaven. (Philippians 4:3; Revelation 3:5; 20: 11-15; 21:27)

linen (LEH-nin) is a type of cloth made from the flax plant. The priests and rich people wore linen clothes. Jesus' body was wrapped in linen when he was buried. Since linen was expensive, it was usually worn on special occasions. (Exodus 28:39; Leviticus 6:10; Esther 8:15; Proverbs 31:24; Matthew 27:59; Revelation 15:6) See also "flax."

lion was a common animal in Bible times. Lions are mentioned more than 100 times in the Bible. They were probably Asian lions. These

lion

are smaller than the African lions. David and Samson each killed a lion. Daniel was saved by God from a den full of lions into which he had been thrown. People thought of lions as being strong and brave. So Jesus was called "the lion of the tribe of Judah." (Judges 14:5-6; 1 Samuel 17:34-37; Psalm 104:21; Proverbs 28:1; Revelation 5:5)

locust (LO-cust) is an insect that looks like a grasshopper. Locusts travel in large groups. They eat crops and other green plants. Lo-

custs were sometimes eaten as food. (Exodus 10:4-19; Deuteronomy 28: 38-42; Joel 1:4; Matthew 3:4)

lord means "master" or one who is in control. Jesus is called Lord because he rules over all the world and universe. Christians serve Jesus as Lord of their lives. (Acts 2:36; 21:

12-14; Romans 10:9; 1 Corinthians 6:11; Colossians 3:17-24)

Lord of heaven's armies is one of the names used for God in the Old Testament. This name tells about God's power. He is in charge of all the angels. It shows that the devil is fighting against God and his armies. But God will win. In some Bibles this name is "Lord of Hosts" or the "Lord Almighty." (1 Samuel 1:11; 1 Chronicles 11:9; Psalm 24:10; Isaiah 6:3-5; Malachi 3:1-17)

Lord of Hosts See "Lord of heaven's armies."

Lord's day is the first day of the week (Sunday, in many countries). Jesus was raised from death on the first day of the week. He told Christians to meet together on this day, too. (Luke 24:1-8; Acts 20:7; Revelation 1:10)

Lord's Prayer is the name often given to the model prayer Jesus taught his followers. (Matthew 6:9-13; Luke 11:1-4)

Lord's Supper is the meal Jesus' followers eat to remember how he died for them. The bread reminds us of his body. The fruit of the vine reminds us of his blood. The Lord's Supper also shows that Jesus came back to life and now lives in heaven with God. (Matthew 26:26-30; Luke 22:14-20; 1 Corinthians 10:17; 11:23-32)

Lot was Abraham's nephew. They traveled together to Canaan. But Lot ended up living in the wicked city of Sodom. So, when the city was about to be destroyed, his family had to run away. They were told not to stop or look back until they got to the mountains. But Lot's wife did look back at Sodom, and God turned her into a pillar of salt. (Genesis 13–14; 19)

lots were sticks, stones or pieces of bone thrown like dice to decide something. Often God controlled the re-

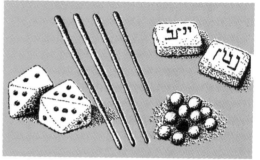

sult of the lots to let the people know what he wanted them to do. (Numbers 26:55-56; Proverbs 18:18; Jonah 1:7; Luke 1:9; 23:34; Acts 1:26)

Lot's wife See "Lot."

love is a strong feeling of affection, loyalty and concern for someone else. God loved us, even when we did not deserve to be loved. The Bible says, "God is love." So the more we know about God, the more we can know love. Christian love means to do good to someone. God loved us so much that he sent his only son Jesus to save us. We love God and other people because he loved us first. (Deuteronomy 6:5; Psalms 17:7; 136:1-26; Matthew 22:37-40; John 3:16; 14:23; Romans 5:5-8; 1 Corinthians 13; 1 John 3:11-18; 4:7-21)

Luke was a non-Jewish doctor who often traveled with the apostle Paul. He was a very educated man. He wrote the books of Luke and Acts in the New Testament. Luke tells many acts of Jesus that are not told in the other three gospels. (Colossians 4:14; 2 Timothy 4:11)

Luke, Gospel of, is the third book in the New Testament. It tells the story of Jesus. It was probably written for non-Jewish people. Luke mentions women and prayer more than the other three gospel writers. The book ends when Jesus returns to heaven. Luke wrote another book called "Acts." In it he continues his story of Jesus by telling what happened to Jesus' followers after Jesus went back to heaven.

Lydia (LID-ee-uh) was a woman from the city of Thyatira who sold purple cloth. Paul met her in the city of Philippi and taught her about Jesus. She and the people who lived in her house were the first people on the continent of Europe to become Christians. (Acts 16:13-15,40)

lyre (LIRE) is a musical instrument with strings. It is similar to a harp,

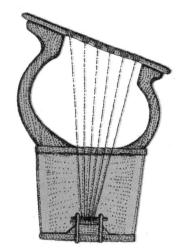

but smaller. (2 Samuel 6:5; 1 Chronicles 15:16-28; Psalms 33:2; 144:9; 150:3)

M

Macedonia (mas-eh-DOH-nee-uh) is a northern part of the country of Greece. Its capital was Thessalonica. Paul had a dream of a man begging him to come to Macedonia to help the people there. The next day Paul left to go to Macedonia to tell them about Jesus. The books of 1 and 2 Thessalonians were letters written to the Christians there. (Acts 16:7-12)

Machpelah (mack-PEE-luh) was the name of the land Abraham bought from Ephron, the Hittite. He bought this field because it had a cave where he could bury his wife, Sarah. Later Abraham, Isaac, Rebekah, Jacob and Leah were also buried there. This cave can still be visited today. (Genesis 23:9-19; 25:9-10; 35:29; 47:38-31; 49:29-33; 50:12-13)

magic (MA-jik) in the Bible means

trying to use the power of evil spirits to make unnatural things happen. God's people were told to stay away from magic. In the New Testament when people became Christians, they burned their books of magic. This magic is not the same as the tricks most magicians do today. They are not really trying to use evil power. They are just entertaining people. (Genesis 41:8; Leviticus 19:26; 20:27; Deuteronomy 18:10-12; Acts 8:9-24; 13:6-8; 19:19)

magnificat (mag-NIFF-eh-kat) is a Latin word that means "praise." This word does not actually appear in the Bible. It is a name sometimes given to the song Mary sang when the angel told her that she would be the mother of the Son of God. (Luke 1:46-55)

mahalath (mah-HAY-lath), or mahalath leannoth, was probably a musical word. It may have been the name of a tune, or it may mean to dance and shout. (Psalms 53; 88)

Malachi (MAL-uh-ky) was a prophet who lived about the time of Nehemiah. He wrote the last book of the Old Testament. The book of Malachi encourages the Jews to obey God and trust him to care for them. He warned them about punishment but also reminded them of God's love.

Manasseh (mah-NASS-uh) was the name of two men in the Old Testament.

Manasseh, son of Hezekiah, was king of Judah for 55 years. But he did not follow his father's example of worshiping God. Manasseh led the people into idol worship. Later, he was taken as a prisoner to Baby-lon. When he came back to Jerusalem, he started serving God. (2 Kings 21:1-17; 2 Chronicles 33:1-20)

Manasseh, son of Joseph, was born in Egypt. His descendants were the tribe of Manasseh. He was the older brother of Ephraim. (Genesis 41:51; 46:20; 48:5,19)

manger (MAIN-jur) is a box where animals are fed. A feeding box in Bible times was usually made out

of stone. Since Jesus was born in a stable, there was no baby bed nearby. So, Mary used a feeding box for his first bed. (Luke 2:6-17)

manna (MAN-ah) means "what is it?" It was the white, sweet-tasting food God gave the people of Israel in the wilderness. It appeared on the ground during the night so they could gather it in the morning. (Exodus 16:13-15; Numbers 11:7-9; Joshua 5:12; Hebrews 9:4)

Manoah (mah-NO-uh) was the father of Samson. An angel told Manoah's wife she would have a son and that he should be treated in a special way. Manoah prayed that the angel would come back and tell them more, and the angel did. Manoah asked the angel his name. See Judges 13:17-18 to find out his unusual answer. Manoah and his wife did not know they were talking to an angel until later. (Judges 13)

Marduk (MAR-dook) was a false god of the Babylonians. Marduk was the chief false god of the city of Babylon. The Babylonians believed that people were evil because Marduk had created them from the blood of an evil god named Kingu that Marduk defeated. The Babylonians also believed that people were created just to be servants of the false gods and to do their "dirty work." But the Bible says God created people like himself. He made people different than any other creature. And God created people to be good, not evil as Marduk claimed. (Genesis 1:26, Jeremiah 50:2)

Mark, sometimes called John Mark, was a cousin to Barnabas. Mark traveled with Paul and Barnabas on part of their first missionary journey. He also wrote the Gospel of Mark. Christians met in the home of Mark's mother, Mary, to pray for Peter to be freed from prison.(Acts 12:12,25; 13:5,13; 15:36-41; Colossians 4:10; 2 Timothy 4:11)

Mark, Gospel of, is the second book of the New Testament. It is the shortest of the four gospels. Many people think it was also the first one written. Mark has been called the "gospel of action" because it tells many things that Jesus did. The other gospels tell more about what he said.

marketplace was usually a large open area inside a city where people came together to sell and buy goods. The marketplace was a busy place and often one of the centers of town life in Bible times. (Matthew 20:3; Mark 7:4; 12:38; Luke 7:32; Acts 16:19) See page 78.

Mars Hill See "Areopagus."

Martha (Mar-thuh) was the sister of Mary and Lazarus. They lived in the village of Bethany, which is very near Jerusalem. Jesus often stayed in their home when he was in that area. Martha and her brother and sister loved Jesus very much. (Luke 10:38-41; John 11:1-39; 12:12)

martyr (MAR-ter) is a Greek word that means "witness." Being a witness means telling what you know about something. Later, martyr came to mean a person who was killed for being a witness. Stephen was the first Christian martyr. He was killed because he told people that Jesus is the Son of God. It is believed that all the apostles, except John, were martyrs for being witnesses of Jesus. (Acts 7:54-60; 12:2; 22:20; Revelation 2:13)

Mary is the name of several women in the New Testament:

Mary Magdalene was from the town of Magdala. She was a follower of Jesus. She watched the men put Jesus' body in the tomb. She was the first person to see Jesus after he came back to life. (Matthew 27:56,61; Mark 15:40, 47; 16:1,9; John 20:1-18)

Mary of Bethany was the sister of Martha and Lazarus. She was a dear friend of Jesus. Mary sat at Jesus' feet and listened to him teach. One time she poured some

M

Marketplace

expensive perfume on his feet and dried them with her hair. (Luke 10:39-42)

Mary, the mother of Jesus, was a Jewish woman whom God chose to give birth to his only Son. This was a great honor and blessing from God. She married a man named Joseph. Mary stood at the foot of the cross when Jesus was killed. (Matthew 1:18-25; Luke 1:27-45; John 19:25-27)

maskil (MAS-kil) is probably a description of the kind of song that some of the Psalms were. It describes 13 of the Psalms. (Psalms 32, 42, 44, 45)

Matthew (MATH-you), also called Levi, was a tax collector. He was 1 of Jesus' 12 apostles. He wrote the Gospel of Matthew. (Matthew 9:9-10; 10:3)

Matthew, Gospel of, is the story of Jesus written for Jewish people. Matthew often shows how Jesus made the Old Testament teachings come true. Matthew tells of many things Jesus taught, such as the Sermon on the Mount. This gospel contains ten parables that are not mentioned anywhere else. The writer's name is not told in the book. But Christians from very early times believed the apostle Matthew wrote it.

Matthias (muh-THY-us) was chosen to be an apostle after Judas Iscariot killed himself for betraying Jesus. (Acts 1:15-26)

Mediterranean Sea (med-ih-teh-RANE-ih-an) is a large sea of water enclosed by the lands of southern Europe, western Asia and northern Africa. It is also called the "Great Sea" or the "Western Sea." (Numbers 34:6-7; Joshua 1:4)

Medes (MEEDS) were the people who lived in Media. It is called Iran today. When the Assyrians captured Israel, they took many of the Jews to the cities of the Medes. The Medes and Persians defeated Babylon when Belshazzar was the ruler. Daniel was put into the lions' den when Darius the Mede could not change a law he had made. (2 Kings 17:6; Ezra 6:2-4; Esther 1:3-19; Daniel 5:28; 6:8-15; 8:20)

medium (MEED-ee-um) means "go-between." This is a person who tries to help living people talk to the spirits of dead people. (Leviticus 19:31; Deuteronomy 18:11; 1 Samuel 28:3-9; 2 Kings 23:24; Isaiah 8:19-20)

Meeting Tent is often called the Tabernacle or Holy Tent. This was the special tent where the Israelites worshiped God. It was used from the time they left Egypt until Solomon built the Temple in Jerusalem. This tent was kept in the middle of their camp to remind them that God was always with them. (Exodus 25–27; 39:32–40:36; Numbers 8; 2 Chronicles 1:3-13; 5:5) See page 80.

Megiddo (meh-GID-oh) was an important Old Testament town in northern Israel. Joshua captured the city from the Canaanites. Solomon made it a place to keep chariots and horses in case of war. In later battles, two kings of Judah (Ahaziah and Josiah) were killed there. Many battles were fought at Megiddo. So, the book of Revelation tells about a great battle between good and evil at "Armageddon," which means "the

M

Meeting Tent

hill of Megiddo." (Joshua 12:21; 1 Kings 9:15-27; 2 Kings 23:29-30; 2 Chronicles 35:22; Revelation 16:16)

Melchizedek (mel-KIZ-ih-dek) means "king of righteousness." He was a priest and king who worshiped God in the time of Abraham. Jesus is now the Christian's king and high priest. In this way, Jesus is a priest and a king like Melchizedek. (Genesis 14:17-24; Hebrews 5:4-10; 7:1-17)

Mene, Mene, Tekel, Parsin (MEE-nee, TEE-kul, PAR-sun) were the words written on the wall by a mysterious hand at Belshazzar's feast. He was upset and called in his wise men to tell him what the words meant. They could probably read the words. But they did not know why they were there or what they meant. Daniel was called in to see if he could give their meaning. God let Daniel know that the words meant Belshazzar would die. He had been evil, and his kingdom was going to be divided. And, it all happened that very night. (Daniel 5) See also "Belshazzar."

Mephibosheth (me-FIB-o-sheth) was the son of Jonathan. He was crippled because a nurse dropped him when he was small. Jonathan was killed when Mephibosheth was only five years old. Later, King David found out where he was. Because Jonathan had been his friend, David wanted to take care of Mephibosheth. So, David allowed him to live at the king's palace. (2 Samuel 4:4; 9:1-13; 16:1-4; 19:24-30)

Merab (MEE-rab) was a daughter of King Saul. He promised David he could marry Merab. But Saul gave Merab to someone else as a wife. He did allow another daughter, Michal, to marry David. (1 Samuel 14:49; 18:17-27)

Merarites (mee-RAY-rites) were the descendants of Merari, a son of Levi. They were one of the three groups of Levites who took care of the Meeting Tent and Temple. (Numbers 3:17, 33-37; 4:29-33; 26:57; 1 Chronicles 23:6,21-23; Ezra 8:18-20)

mercy (MUR-see) is kindness and forgiveness. God had mercy on us. He sent his only Son, Jesus, to die on the cross for our sins. We, too, are taught to have mercy on other people. God says he will be as merciful to us as we are to others. (Genesis 43:14; 2 Samuel 24:14; Matthew 5:7; Romans 11:32; James 2:13; 5:11; 1 Peter 2:10)

mercy seat See "lid on the Holy Box."

Mesha (MEE-shuh) was an evil king of Moab. He fought against the kings of Judah and Israel. Once the Israelites were winning a battle so Mesha sacrificed his son as a burnt offering to his false god. The Israelites did not want to be part of such evil. So, they quit fighting and went home. (2 Kings 3:4-27)

Messiah (muh-SYE-uh) is a Hebrew word for "anointed one" or "one appointed or chosen by God." The Greek word for Messiah is "Christ." Christians believe that Jesus is the Messiah or Christ. (John 1:41; 4:25)

Methuselah (meh-THOO-zeh-lah) lived longer than anyone else in the Bible. He died at the age of 969. Methuselah was the son of Enoch and the grandfather of Noah. (Genesis 5:21-27)

Micah (MY-cuh) is the name of a prophet and the book he wrote. He told the people of Israel and Judah about their sins. Some people were pretending to love God, but they were not really serving him. They cheated and acted dishonestly. But Micah also had some good news. He said a great ruler for God would come from Bethlehem. And that's where Jesus was born many years later. (Micah 2:1-3; 3:1-4; 5:2-5)

Micaiah (mi-KAY-uh) was a prophet of God. He lived when Ahab was king. Ahab asked many prophets whether or not he would win the next battle he was to fight. All except Micaiah told him "yes." But Micaiah said, "You will not win. God is going to punish you." This made Ahab angry, and he put Micaiah in prison. But Micaiah was right, and Ahab was killed. (1 Kings 22:8-28; 2 Chronicles 18)

Michael (MY-kul) is the archangel or leader of God's angels. He works to protect God's people against Satan. Once Daniel was afraid because of a frightening vision he had seen. Read Daniel 10:18-19 and see what Michael said to make Daniel feel better. (Daniel 10:10-21; Jude 1:9; Revelation 12:7)

Michal (MY-kul) was a daughter of King Saul. He used her to try to kill David. Saul told David he could marry Michal if he killed 100 Philistines. He thought the Philistines would kill David before he could kill them. But actually David killed 200 Philistines. So, Saul had to let David and Michal marry. Later, Michal saved David's life when Saul was after him again. (1 Samuel 18:20-29; 19:11-17)

Michmash (MIK-mash) is a hilly area about seven miles northeast of Jerusalem. The Philistine armies were camped there once when Saul was king. Jonathan and the man who carried his armor climbed up the hill to fight them. They were so successful that the Philistines panicked and made so much noise that the rest of the Israelites attacked. So, the Philistines were forced back that day. Many years later, when the Assyrians came to attack, they went

M

through Michmash. (1 Samuel 13: 23–14:23; Ezra 2:27; Nehemiah 7: 31; Isaiah 10:28)

Midian (MID-ee-un) was a son of Abraham. His descendants were called Midianites. They lived in the desert area called Midian. Moses' wife was a Midianite. The Midianites helped the Israelites when they were traveling toward the promised land. Later they were enemies. The Midianites rode camels and often attacked the Israelites. But God helped Gideon defeat them. (Genesis 25:1-6; Exodus 2:15-21; 18:1-11; Judges 6–7)

miktam (MIK-tam) is a kind of song. It is probably a description of some of the Psalms. It may mean that it is a sad song or a song about danger. (Psalms 16; 56–60)

mildew (MIL-doo) is a growth that appears on things that have been damp for a long time. (Leviticus 13:47-59; 14:33-54)

millstones were huge stones used for grinding grain into flour or meal. There was a large stone on the bottom and a smaller one on top. The grain was put between the stones. Then the top stone was turned or pushed against the bottom one. This crushed the grain into smaller and smaller pieces. Then it could be used for cooking. Sometimes millstones were small enough to be used by one or two women. Others were larger and had to be turned by hitching an animal, like an ox or donkey, to the top stone and making the animal walk in a circle. This was probably what the Philistines made Samson do. (Deuteronomy 24:6; Judges 9:53; 16:21; Revelation 18:21-22)

minister (MIN-i-ster) means "servant." It also means one who lives serving God and others. Christians are taught to minister to each other and to non-Christians. (Romans 15:16)

miracle (MEER-ih-k'l) is a Latin word that means "wonderful thing." It is a great event which can be done only by God's help. Miracles are special signs to show God's power. In the Old Testament God used miracles to rescue his people. Jesus did miracles to prove that he was God's Son. The Bible tells us of many miracles. Sick people were healed, blind people were given sight, crippled people were able to walk and people could speak languages they had never studied. Sometimes people were even brought back to life after they had died. The best miracle was Jesus' coming back to life after he was killed on the cross. (Nehemiah 9:17; Psalm 77:11, 14; Matthew 28:5-7; Luke 23:8; John 2:1-11; 3:2; 20:30-31; Acts 4:16-22; 8:13)

Miriam (MEER-ee-um) was the sister of Moses and Aaron. She must have been the one who watched the baby Moses when he was put in a basket in the Nile River to hide him from the king of Egypt. Later, Miriam made up a song to celebrate the Israelites' crossing of the Red Sea. She became a leader of the Israelites. When she died, she was buried at Kadesh. (Exodus 2:4-8; 15:20-21; Numbers 12:1-15; 20:1; Micah 6:4)

Mizpah (MIZ-pah) or Mizpeh means "watch tower." This was the name of several places in the Bible.

Mizpah was where Jacob and Laban made a pile of stones to remind them that they had agreed not to be angry with each other. It also reminded them that God would be watching over them. (Genesis 31:44-49)

Mizpah was a city a few miles north of Jerusalem. Samuel often went there when he was judge. This was where he introduced Saul as their king. (1 Samuel 7:5-16; 10:17; 2 Kings 25:23)

Moab (MO-ab) was the country on the east side of the Dead Sea. The land is high and flat. Several times over the years the Moabites fought with the Israelites. Ruth was from Moab. Her story took place during a time of peace. About 850 B.C. Israel and Judah came together and defeated Moab. It was never a strong country again. (Numbers 22:1–25:9; Judges 3:12-25; 2 Kings 3:4-27)

Molech (MO-lek) was a false god of the Canaanite people. Those who worshiped Molech often sacrificed their own children to him by burning them on altars. (Leviticus 18:21; 20:1-5; 2 Kings 23:10; Jeremiah 32:35)

money is something people use to pay for goods or services. Many kinds of money were used in Bible days— gold, silver and copper. The Bible teaches that money should be used for good things, like caring for your family and helping others. But to love money can cause many evil things to happen. (Psalm 15:5; Proverbs 13:11; Isaiah 55:1-2; Matthew 10:9; 22:17-21; 1 Timothy 6:10)

money changers were people who traded money from other countries for Jewish money. Jews were supposed to pay a Temple tax each year. And it had to be paid with a certain Jewish coin. If a person had money from somewhere else, he could trade it for the right Jewish coin. But some of these money changers cheated people. Their tables were set up in the Temple courtyard for non-Jews. So, besides cheating, they were keeping non-Jews from being able to pray there. When Jesus saw what was happening, he became angry and ran them out of the Temple. (Matthew 21:12; Mark 11:15; John 2:13-15)

Mordecai (MOR-deh-kye) and Esther are the heroes of the book of Esther. Mordecai was one of the Jews who had probably been born in captivity in Persia. He helped save the life of King Xerxes. Later, he worked with Esther to save the Jews when Haman was trying to kill them all. (Esther 2:5–10:3) See also "Haman" and "Esther."

Moriah (moh-RYE-uh) was the land

M

Money of Bible Times

Denarius of Tiberius
16¢

A Mite = ⅛¢

A Silver
Tetradrachm

Coin of
Herod Philip

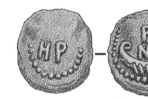

Denarius of Augustus Caesar
16¢

Coin by
Pontius Pilate

Copper Coin of
Herod the Great

Coin of
Herod Antipas

Coin of
Herod Archelaus

Mite of Coponius
⅛¢

Shekel of AD 2
64¢

Ancient Greek
Coin

Macedonian
Coin

where God told Abraham to take his son Isaac to sacrifice him. But God stopped Abraham before he killed Isaac. Many years later, Solomon built the Temple on Mount Moriah. These two Moriahs may have been the same place. (Genesis 22:2; 2 Chronicles 3:1)

mortar (MORE-tar) has two meanings:

It can be a stone bowl where grain is ground into flour by pounding. Manna was ground up this way. (Numbers 11:8; Proverbs 27:22)

Mortar is also the sticky material that holds bricks together. It was often made of mud or clay. (Genesis 11:3; Exodus 1:14; Isaiah 41:25)

Moses (MO-zez) in Hebrew means "saved from the water." Moses led God's people out of the land of Egypt where they had been slaves for 400 years. Moses wrote the first five books of the Old Testament. On Mount Sinai God gave to Moses the law for the Israelite people. It is called "the Law of Moses." (Exodus 2–40; Numbers 1–26; Deuteronomy 27–34; John 1:17,45; 3:14; Hebrews 11:23-24; Revelation 15:3)

Most Holy Place was the inner and most special room in the Meeting Tent and the Temple. The Box of the Agreement was kept there. Only the high priest could go into this room, and he could enter only once a year. This was when he sprinkled blood on the lid of the Holy Box to remind the people that their sins needed to be forgiven. (Exodus 26:33-34; Leviticus 16:2-20; 1 Kings 6:16-35; Hebrews 9:3-25)

Mount of Olives is a hill covered with olive trees near Jerusalem. The garden of Gethsemane is on one side of the Mount of Olives. Jesus was praying there when the Roman soldiers came to arrest him. Some of the same olive trees that were in the garden when Jesus was on earth may still be there today. (2 Samuel 15:30; Luke 22:39-52; Acts 1:12)

Mount Zion (ZI-on) at first meant one of the hills on which Jerusalem was built. Later Zion became another name for the whole city of Jerusalem. In the New Testament, Zion is also used as a name for heaven. (Psalms 48:2,11; 74:2; 78:68; Obadiah 17; Hebrews 12:22)

mourning (MORN-ing) means showing sadness, especially when someone has died. In Bible times people showed their sadness in many ways: tearing their clothes, wearing sackcloth (rough clothing), dressing in black, taking off all jewelry, shaving their heads, fasting, or covering part

M

of the face. Sometimes there was an official period of mourning for a famous person. This time of sorrow was 7 days for Saul, 30 days for Moses and 70 days for Jacob. (Genesis 37:29,34; 50:3; Leviticus 10:6; 13:45; Deuteronomy 21:12-13; 34:8;

1 Samuel 31:13; 2 Samuel 1:12; 13:9; 14:2)

myrrh (MUR) was a sweet-smelling liquid taken from certain trees and shrubs. It was used as a perfume and as a pain reliever. It was one of the gifts the wise men gave Jesus when he was born. (Genesis 37:25; 43:11; Proverbs 7:17; Matthew 2:11; Mark 15:23; John 19:39)

mystery (MIH-ster-ee) in the Bible means a secret truth. It is a truth that once was a secret. Now God has let it be known to everyone who wants to know. For example, our bodies will change when Jesus returns. People in Old Testament days didn't know about that secret. God has now told us all about it in the New Testament. (1 Corinthians 15: 51-54; Ephesians 3:3-6; Colossians 1:26-27; 1 Timothy 3:16)

N

Naaman (NAY-uh-mun) was a commander of the Aramean army. He had a harmful skin disease. He heard that Elisha, an Israelite prophet, could heal him. So, Naaman went to see him. Elisha told him to go wash in the Jordan River seven times. At first, he didn't want to do it. Finally, he did and his skin became as healthy as a child's. (2 Kings 5)

Naboth (NAY-both) lived in Jezreel and owned a nice vineyard. King Ahab wanted to buy it. But Naboth wouldn't sell it because it had been in his family for many years. So, Ahab's evil wife Jezebel had Naboth killed. God then sent Elijah to tell Ahab, "In the same place that Naboth died, you will also die." And that is exactly what happened to Ahab and Jezebel. (1 Kings 21:1-29; 22:34-38; 2 Kings 9:30-37)

Nahum (NAY-hum) is the name of a prophet and the short book he wrote. His message was aimed at Assyria and its capital city, Nineveh. He said they would be defeated because they had been evil, proud and cruel. Later, the Babylonians, Scythians and Medes did destroy Nineveh as Nahum had said. (Nahum 1–3)

names in the Bible were very important. People were given names to show many things. One of Rebekah's sons was born with a lot of hair. So, he was named Esau, which means "hairy." Sometimes God gave people names as a reminder. Sarah laughed when God said she would have a son. So, God said the son's name would be Isaac, which sounds like the word for "laughed." Isaac's name would always remind Sarah not to laugh when God says something.

Several people's names were changed. Abraham, Jacob and Paul all had a special meeting with the Lord. And all their names were changed as signs of the changes in their lives. Some people got new names because of something good they did. Gideon tore down the idol of the false god Baal. So he was called Jerub-Baal. That means, "let Baal fight against him."

Parents often gave children names hoping they would grow up to be like their name. For example, Ehud means "strong" and Obadiah means "servant of the Lord." (Genesis 18: 10-15; 32:28; Judges 6:32; Acts 4:36)

Naomi (nay-OH-me) was the mother-in-law of Ruth. She was a Jew who had moved to the foreign land of Moab. There her sons and husband died. So she decided to return to Israel. But Ruth, her Moabite daughter-in-law, came too. In Bethlehem, Naomi helped Ruth meet Boaz. Boaz then married Ruth and took care of Naomi. (Ruth 1–4)

Naphtali (NAF-tuh-lye) was the sixth son of Jacob. His descendants were the tribe of Naphtali. Their land was west of Lake Galilee. This area was known as Galilee in Jesus' time. (Genesis 30:7-8; Joshua 19: 32-39; 1 Kings 15:20)

nard was an expensive perfume. It cost so much because it had to be imported from India. (Song of Solomon 4:13; Mark 14:3; John 12:3)

Nathan (NAY-thun) was the name of several people in the Old Testament. But the most important was a prophet during the time of David and Solomon. He told David that his son Solomon would build the Temple. Once, David had Bathsheba's husband killed. Then he married her. Nathan told him it was wrong. Also, Nathan helped make sure that Solomon took David's place as king. (2 Samuel 7:1-17; 12:1-25; 1 Kings 1; 1 Chronicles 29:29; 2 Chronicles 9:29)

Nathanael (nuh-THAN-yul) was 1 of Jesus' 12 apostles. He is mentioned only in the Gospel of John. He is probably the same person called Bartholomew in the other gospels. Philip introduced Nathanael to Jesus. (John 1:43-51)

Nazarene (NAZ-uh-reen) is a person from the town of Nazareth. Jesus grew up in Nazareth and was called a Nazarene. Sometimes Christians also were called Nazarenes, since they followed Jesus. (Matthew 2:23; Acts 24:5)

Nazareth (NAZ-uh-reth) was the city in Galilee where Jesus grew up. When he went back there to preach, the people at first liked what he said. But soon they became angry at him and tried to push him off a cliff. (Matthew 2:23; Mark 1:9; Luke 4: 16-30; John 1:45-46)

Nazirite (NAZ-e-rite) was a Jewish person who made a special promise to God. He was to serve God by following special rules. Samson and Samuel were Nazirites. (Numbers 6:1-21; Judges 13:7; 16:17)

Nebo (NEE-boh) was the name of a Babylonian god. He was thought to be the god of writing and the son of Bel. (Isaiah 46:1)

Nebo was also the name of the mountain where Moses died, as well as a town nearby. (Numbers 32:3; Deuteronomy 34:1; Isaiah 15:2)

Nebuchadnezzar (neb-you-kud-NEZ-zur) was a Babylonian king. He captured and destroyed Jerusalem and took Daniel and others as captives to Babylon. (2 Kings 24–25; 2 Chronicles 36; Daniel 1–5)

Nebuzaradan (NEB-u-ZAR-ah-dan) was the commander of Nebuchadnezzar's army. He was in charge of burning the important buildings and tearing down the walls of Jerusalem. He also took many of the people as prisoners to Babylon. Nebuzaradan set Jeremiah the prophet free. (2 Kings 25:8-12; Jeremiah 39:9-14; 40:1-6)

Necho (NECK-o) was king of Egypt from 609 to 594 B.C. He attacked Judah, and King Josiah was killed. A few years later, Nebuchadnezzar defeated Necho and forced his army out of Judah. (2 Kings 23:29-37; 2 Chronicles 35:20-27; 36:1-4; Jeremiah 46:2)

Nehemiah (NEE-uh-MY-uh) is the main character of the book of Nehemiah. At first he worked for King Artaxerxes of Persia. This was many years after Jerusalem had been destroyed. Nehemiah got permission to go help the Jews rebuild the city walls of Jerusalem. He was such a good leader that they finished the job in only 52 days. The last part of the book tells how Nehemiah served as governor of Jerusalem. He made sure the people knew God's Word and obeyed it. (Nehemiah 1–12)

neighbor (NAY-bur) in the Bible means the people around us. God said, "Love your neighbor as you love yourself." But some people in Jesus' time thought neighbor meant only certain kinds of people. That's why Jesus told the story of the good Samaritan. He showed that our neighbor is anyone we have a chance to help. (Exodus 20:17; Leviticus 19:18; Proverbs 3:29; 11:12; 14:21; Matthew 19:19; Luke 10:29-37)

Nephilim (NEF-eh-lim) were a group of people who were famous for being large and strong. The ten spies who were afraid to enter Canaan had seen the Nephilim who lived there. (Genesis 6:4; Numbers 13:33)

New Moon was a Jewish feast held on the first day of the month. It was celebrated with animal sacrifices and the blowing of trumpets. It was a way for the Israelites to dedicate the month to the Lord. (Numbers 10:10; 28:14; 1 Samuel 20:5,24; Psalm 81:3; Ezekiel 46:3-6; Colossians 2:16)

New Testament is the name for the last 27 books of the Bible. The first 4 books (Matthew, Mark, Luke and John) are called gospels. They tell the Good News about the life of Jesus. The fifth book is called Acts. It tells what Jesus' followers did in the first 30 years after he went back to heaven. Next are 21 letters written to help early Christians. The last book is Revelation. It is a vision God gave to John to let him know what would happen in the future. "Testament" means "agreement." The New Testament tells about Jesus and the new agreement between God and man. It shows God's way of making people right with him.

Nicodemus (nick-uh-DEE-mus) means "conqueror (master) of the people." He was an important Jewish ruler and teacher. One night he came to talk to Jesus, and Jesus taught him about spiritual life. Later, Nicodemus helped Joseph of Arimathea bury Jesus. (John 3:1-21; 7:44-53; 19:38-42)

Nile River is a river in Africa more than 2500 miles long. It starts in central Africa and flows into the Mediterranean Sea in the land of Egypt. The river keeps Egypt from

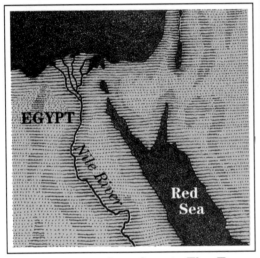

EGYPT

Nile River

Red Sea

being a complete desert. The Egyptians depended on the Nile so much they started thinking of it as a god. One of the kings of Egypt had Hebrew babies thrown into the Nile to kill them. One of the ten punishments God sent to the Egyptians was turning the Nile into blood. (Genesis 41; Exodus 1:22; 2:3-10; 7:17-25; 8:1-15)

Nineveh (NIN-eh-vuh) was one of the oldest and most important cities in the world. People were already living there more than 4000 years before Jesus was born. For many years it was the capital of Assyria. Nineveh was the city where Jonah did not want to preach. It was destroyed in 612 B.C. by the Babylonians, Medes and Scythians. (Genesis 10:11; 2 Kings 19:36-37; Jonah 1:2; 3:2-3; Nahum 1:1)

Noah (NO-uh) and his family were the only people of their time who served God. So God told them about the great flood that was coming. They built a large boat (often called an ark) about 450 feet long. Noah's family and every kind of animal were saved to start life on earth all over again. (Genesis 6–9; 1 Peter 3:20) See also "ark, Noah's."

Noah's ark See "ark, Noah's."

Nob was a town where priests lived during the days of King Saul. The Meeting Tent was kept there for awhile. When David was running away from Saul, he went to Nob. There Ahimelech the priest helped David. No one knows exactly where Nob was. But we do know that it was on a hill near Jerusalem. (1 Samuel 21; Nehemiah 11:32; Isaiah 10:32)

Numbers is the fourth book of the Old Testament. The name comes from the two numberings mentioned in the book. The Israelites were counted at the beginning and again at the end of the 40 years in the wilderness. The Jews' earliest name for this book was "Wilderness," because Numbers tells of their travels in the wilderness until they got to the edge of the promised land. It also gives many laws and rules that the Israelites were to follow.

N

O

Obadiah (oh-buh-DYE-uh) is the shortest book in the Old Testament. A prophet named Obadiah gave God's message to the Edomites. He said they would be punished for not helping their neighbors, the Israelites. The Edomites even seemed to enjoy seeing the Israelites suffer. There is also good news in the book: God's people will come back to their homeland.

obedience (o-BEE-dee-ence) or **obey** means doing what we are asked or told to do. Jesus showed us that obeying God is a part of loving him. (Deuteronomy 4:30; 1 Samuel 15:19-22; Nehemiah 1:5-9; Ephesians 6:1; Philippians 2:8; 2 Thessalonians 1:8; Hebrews 5:8-9; 13:17)

Og (AHG) was the king of Bashan. This was a land the Israelites captured on their way to the promised land. Og was ruler over 60 cities. He was a giant. His bed was 13 feet long. (Deuteronomy 3:1-11; Nehemiah 9:21-22)

oil in the Bible usually means olive oil. It was used in many ways, such as cooking, medicine and burning in lamps. Also oil was poured on a person's head to anoint him. This meant he had been chosen for a special job, such as being a king or prophet. Oil was also rubbed on the skin to make it softer. (Ruth 3:3; 1 Samuel 10:1; 1 Kings 17:12-16; Psalm 23:5; Matthew 25:1-13; Luke 10:34) See also "anoint."

ointment See "perfume."

Old Testament is the name for the first 39 books of the Bible. It is the story of how God made everything good. But man spoiled it by sinning. The Old Testament tells how God worked with people while preparing for the coming of Jesus. There are books of law, history, poetry and prophecy. The laws of the Old Testament were for the Jews. But Christians can learn much from the Old Testament about God and his care for his creation. Paul wrote this about the Old Testament: "Everything that was written in the past was written to teach us, so that we could have hope. That hope comes from the patience and encouragement that the Scriptures give us." (Romans 15:4)

Olives, Mount of, See "Mount of Olives."

omega See "Alpha and Omega."

Omri (OM-rih) was a strong, but evil, king of Israel. He was an army commander when King Elah died. But his soldiers made him king. Two other men were also trying to be king at that time. Omri's side won out. He built and named the city of Samaria. But he kept the people worshiping idols. (1 Kings 16:8-28)

Onesimus (oh-NES-ih-mus) was the

slave of a Christian named Philemon in the city of Colossae. Onesimus ran away from Philemon to the city of Rome. There he met the apostle Paul and became a Christian. Paul told him to return to Philemon. The book of Philemon is the letter Paul sent back to Philemon with Onesimus. Paul asked Philemon to treat Onesimus kindly, as he would any other Christian brother. (Colossians 4:9; Philemon)

Onesiphorus (OH-nih-SIF-uh-russ) was a Christian friend of Paul who lived in Ephesus. Paul especially appreciated it when Onesiphorus came to visit him in prison. (2 Timothy 1:16-18; 4:19)

onyx (AHN-ix) is a precious stone with layers of black and white running through it. Two onyx stones were put on Aaron's holy vest. Each one had the names of six different tribes of Israel carved on it. Onyx stones also decorated the Temple Solomon built. (Exodus 25:7; 28:9-11; 39:6,13; 1 Chronicles 29:2)

Ophir (OH-fur) was a land known for its gold and beautiful trees. Solomon and Hiram sent ships to Ophir to bring these things back. No one knows where Ophir was. It may have been in India or Africa. (1 Kings 9:28; 10:11; 1 Chronicles 29:4)

ovens in Bible times were made out of clay. They were like large jars or barrels. Fire was built in the

bottom. Bread dough was usually pushed against the hot inner walls. But sometimes the dough was put on the hot rocks in the bottom. (Exodus 8:3; Leviticus 2:4; Hosea 7:4)

P

palace (PAL-uhs) is the house of a king or queen. It was usually a large fancy house. Many palaces had open courtyards in the middle. The rooms were built around it. David used cedar wood, carpenters and stone cutters from the city of Tyre to build his palace. Solomon also built a new palace. It took 13 years to finish it. (2 Samuel 5:7-12; 1 Kings 7:1-12)

palm trees were very valuable in Bible lands. The palm gave dates for food and wood for building. The leaves were used to make ropes and mats. The seeds were food for cam-

els. The palm is tall with long, fan-shaped branches growing out of the top. One time the people of Jerusalem used palm branches to honor Jesus as he entered the city. (Exodus 15:27; Leviticus 23:40; Deuteronomy 34:3; Judges 1:16; Nehemiah 8:15; John 12:12-13)

papyrus (puh-PY-rus) is a tall reed plant that grows in swampy places. It was used to make something like paper. Strips were glued together to make a scroll to write on. The ear-

liest copies of the New Testament were written on papyrus. Papyrus plants were also used to make small boats. The basket that baby Moses was put in may have been made of papyrus. (Job 8:11; Isaiah 18:2)

parable (PARE-uh-b'l) is a story that teaches a lesson by comparing two things. Jesus often used parables to teach the people. Some examples of parables can be found in Mark 12:1-12, Luke 10:29-37 and Luke 15:1-31.

paradise (PARE-uh-dice) means "garden." It is a happy place where God's people go when they die. (Luke 23:43; 2 Corinthians 12:3-4)

Paran (PAY-ran) was a desert area between Egypt and Canaan. This was where Hagar and Ishmael were sent to live. The Israelites camped here on the way to Canaan. The twelve spies were sent out while they were camped in Paran. (Genesis 21:20; Numbers 10:12; 12:16; 13:1-26)

parchment (PARCH-ment) was a kind of writing material. It was made from the skin of sheep or goats. The

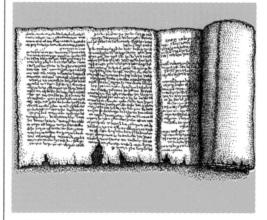

Old Testament was often copied on rolls of parchment. (2 Timothy 4:13)

Passover Feast (PASS-o-ver FEEST)

was an important holy day for the Jews in the spring of each year. They ate a special meal on this day to remind them that God had freed them from being slaves in Egypt. Jesus was killed at Passover time. (Exodus 12:27; Numbers 9; Joshua 5:10; Matthew 26:2,17-19)

patience (PAY-shentz) means to handle pain or difficult times calmly and without complaining. A patient person does not get upset easily or by little things that go wrong. Job was known as a very patient man because he continued to love God even when everything went wrong in his life. (Job; Luke 8:15; Romans 5:3; James 1:3)

Patmos (PAT-mus) is a small, rocky island in the Aegean Sea between the countries of Greece and Turkey. It is called "Patino" today. The apostle John was sent to this island as punishment for being a Christian. There God showed John what to write to the seven churches of Asia. We call this writing the book of Revelation. (Revelation 1:9)

Paul is the Roman name for "Saul." Saul was a Jew, born in the city of Tarsus. He studied under Gamaliel, a famous teacher of God's law. At first, Paul tried to destroy Christ's church by putting Christians in jail and killing them. But Jesus appeared to him and changed his life completely. He was then called Paul. And he became an apostle and a great servant of God. He traveled to many countries, teaching about Jesus. Paul wrote many of the books of the New Testament as letters to Christians in different cities, such as Romans, Colossians and Corinthians. (Acts 7:58-60; 9:1-31; Philippians 3:5-7)

peace in the Bible comes from understanding that we are right with God. This helps put us right with the people around us also. Paul begins his letters by wishing his readers peace. In other words, he wants them to know that they are right with God and everyone else. This gives us a strong feeling of well-being and happiness. (Psalms 4:8; 85:8-10; Romans 5:1; Ephesians 2:14-18; 2 Thessalonians 3:16)

pearl (PURL) is a valuable gem that is formed inside an oyster shell.

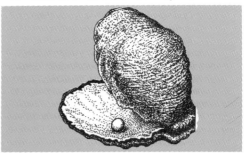

(Matthew 7:6; 13:46; 1 Timothy 2:9; Revelation 21:21)

Pekah (PEE-kuh) was an evil king of Israel. He killed Pekahiah who was the king before him. After taking over, he attacked Judah. But the Assyrians helped Judah and captured part of Israel. Pekah was then killed by Hoshea. (2 Kings 15:25–16:9; Isaiah 7–8)

Pekahiah (peck-uh-HI-uh) was an evil king of Israel. He was murdered by Pekah, who took his place. Pekahiah ruled for only two years. (2 Kings 15:23-26)

Pelethites (PELL-eh-thites) and the

Kerethites were the bodyguards for King David. A man named Benaiah was their commander. (2 Samuel 15:18-22; 20:7,23)

Peninnah (puh-NIN-uh) means "ruby." She was a wife of Elkanah. She made fun of Hannah for not having any children. (1 Samuel 1: 1-7) See also "Hannah."

Word Clues

pente
is a Greek word that means "five." It is often connected to other Greek words, such as in "Pentateuch," which are the first *five* books of the Old Testament. It is also in "Pentecost," which was *fifty* days after the Passover Feast. What other words can you think of that include "pente"?

Pentateuch (PEN-tuh-tuke) is a Greek word that means "five books." It is a name for the first five books of the Old Testament: Genesis, Exodus, Leviticus, Numbers and Deuteronomy. This word does not actually appear in the Bible.

Pentecost (PEN-tee-cost) means "fifty." Pentecost was a Jewish feast day celebrating the summer harvest. It took place 50 days after the Passover Feast. The apostles began telling the Good News on Pentecost after Jesus died. (Acts 2; 20:16; 1 Corinthians 16:8)

perfume (per-FUME) is a pleasant-smelling substance or liquid. Perfume is often made from flowers. (Exodus 30:35-37; Proverbs 27:9; Isaiah 57:9)

Pergamum (PER-guh-mum) was a town in the Roman province of Asia. This area is now called Turkey. It was known for its worship of false gods. One of the letters to the seven churches in the book of Revelation was to Pergamum. (Revelation 2: 12-17)

persecute (PUR-seh-cute) means to hurt people. Christians in the New Testament times were often persecuted. Saul persecuted Christians by dragging them from their homes, putting them in jail and killing them. (Matthew 5:11-12; Acts 8:1-4; Galatians 6:12; 1 Peter 3:13-15)

perseverance (pur-seh-VEER-ence) means "not giving up." We are to keep on doing what is right, even when life gets rough. One way to do this is to learn about the lives of people in the Bible. Those mentioned in Hebrews 11 are good examples of people who kept on even when they had problems. (Matthew 24:13; Luke 21:19; 1 Corinthians 15:58; Galatians 6:9; Ephesians 6: 18; Hebrews 12:1)

Persia (PUR-zhuh) was the name of a powerful country during the last years of the Old Testament. This land is called Iran today. The Medes and Persians captured Babylon when Daniel was there. The Persian king, Cyrus, allowed the Jews to go back and rebuild the walls of Jerusalem. A Jewish girl named Esther became queen to the Persian king, Ahasuerus. The Persians were later defeated by the Greeks. (2 Chronicles 36:20-23; Ezra 1:1-8; Daniel 5:25-28; 6:8) See map on page 7.

Peter (PEE-ter) was a fisherman. He and his brother, Andrew, were the first two apostles Jesus chose. He was first named Simon, but Jesus changed his name to Cephas, which means "rock" in Aramaic. In Greek the name is Peter. Peter, James and John were Jesus' closest friends. Peter was the first to tell the Good News of Jesus to the non-Jewish people. Later in his life Peter wrote the New Testament books of 1 and 2 Peter. He probably died as a martyr for Christ. (Matthew 14:25-33; 16:13-18; Mark 14:27-39; Luke 22:54-62; John 20:1-6; Acts 3:1-26; 10:1-48)

Peter, letters of, were written to Christians who were being punished for believing in Jesus. Peter encouraged them to remember what God had done for them. He said Jesus had to suffer and they would have to suffer, too. Near the end of 1 Peter he said, "Yes, you will suffer for a short time. But after that God will make everything right." Second Peter was written to help Christians who were confused by false teaching. Peter especially reminded them that Jesus was definitely coming back someday.

pharaoh (FAY-row) was the title given to the kings of Egypt. The word first meant "great house," meaning the palace where the king lived. Later it became the title of the king who lived in the great house. Pharaoh is also called "king of Egypt." (Genesis 40–47; Exodus 1–14; 2 Kings 23:29)

Pharisees (FARE-ih-seez) means "the separate people." They were a Jewish religious group who followed the religious laws and customs very strictly. Jesus often spoke against the Pharisees for their religious teachings and traditions. Many of the Pharisees did not like Jesus because he did not follow all of

pharaoh

P

their rules. (Matthew 5:20; 23:23-36; Mark 7:1-13; Luke 18:9-14)

Word Clues

phil
is a Greek word that means "loving" or "fond of." So, in the Bible, "Philip" means "loving horses." "Philemon" means "affectionate." And the city called "Philadelphia" means "brotherly love."

Philadelphia (fill-uh-DEL-fee-uh) means "brotherly love." It was the name of a city in the country we call Turkey today. One of the seven letters to churches in the book of Revelation went to Philadelphia. The Christians there had not been afraid to speak about Jesus. (Revelation 3:7-13)

Philemon (fih-LEE-mun) was a Christian in the city of Colossae. Paul wrote Philemon about his runaway slave, Onesimus. The church at Colossae probably met in Philemon's home. (Philemon 1-25)

Philip (FIL-ip) was the name of several men in the New Testament:

Philip, the apostle, was from the city of Bethsaida and was a friend of Peter and Andrew. He brought Nathanael to Jesus. (Matthew 10: 2-3; John 1:43-48; 12:21-22; 14:8-9)

Philip, the evangelist, was a Greek-speaking Jew. He was one of the seven men chosen to serve in the church in Jerusalem. Later, he preached the Good News in many places. (Acts 6:1-6; 8:5-40; 21:8-9)

Philip, the tetrarch (ruler), was the son of Herod I and Cleopatra. He built the city of Caesarea Philippi. (Luke 3:1)

Philippi (fih-LIP-eye) was a city in the northeast part of Greece, on the main road from Rome to Asia. It was one of the first cities in Europe Paul visited on his journeys. While he was in a Roman prison, Paul wrote a letter to the Christians in Philippi. The letter is the book of Philippians in the New Testament. The city was named for the Greek ruler Philip of Macedonia, who lived about 300 years before Christ was born. (Acts 16:11-40; Philippians 1:1-8; 4:14-18)

Philippians (fih-LIP-ee-unz) was a letter written by the apostle Paul to the church in Philippi. Paul was in prison when he wrote it. He thanked the Philippians for the ways they had helped him in the past. He also let them know that being in prison had not kept him from telling people about Jesus. Paul also told them to work together and to be full of joy.

Philistines (FIL-ih-steens) were Israel's enemy for many years. They had five strong cities near the Mediterranean Sea: Ashdod, Ashkelon, Ekron, Gath and Gaza. They worshiped several false gods. They were finally defeated by the Egyptians. (Judges 15–16; 1 Samuel 4:1-10; 6–7; 17–18; 1 Chronicles 18:1)

Phinehas (FIN-ee-us) was the name of two priests in the Old Testament.

Phinehas was the son of Eli. See "Hophni and Phinehas."

Phinehas, son of Eleazar, was a grandson of Aaron. He was in the wilderness with Moses and the Israelites. To stop a sickness God had sent to the Israelites as punishment, he put to death two people who were doing wrong. (Numbers 25:1-13; 31:6)

Phoenicia (foh-NEE-shuh) was an old name for the land on the east coast of the Mediterranean Sea. We call it Lebanon today. Tyre and Sidon were the most important cities. The Phoenicians were famous for their skill in ship building and sea travel. Jezebel was the daughter of a Phoenician king. (1 Kings 16:31)

phylactery (fih-LAK-tur-ee) See "box of Scriptures."

Pilate, Pontius, (PIE-lut, PON-shus) means "armed with a spear." Pilate was the Roman governor of Judea from A.D. 26 to 36. The Jews who wanted Jesus killed brought him to Pilate. He did not find Jesus guilty of any crime. But Pilate allowed the Jews to crucify Jesus because he was afraid of the people. (Luke 13:1; 23:1-52; Acts 3:13; 4:27; 1 Timothy 6:13)

pillar (PILL-ur) was a large stone that was set upright. Pillars were used to remember something important that happened at that place. For example, Jacob set up a pillar to re-

member the place where he dreamed about the ladder to heaven. But pillars could also be used in a bad way. Some people used pillars to worship false gods. Asa was a good king because he smashed the pillars honoring false gods. Pillar is also the name for the tall columns of stone that hold up the roof of a building. (Genesis 28:18-22; Exodus 23:24; Judges 16: 25-30; 2 Kings 17:10; 2 Chronicles 14:3)

pillar of cloud and fire was the way God led the Israelites in the desert. There was a pillar of cloud in the daytime. At night it was a pillar of fire. This showed them which way to go and where to stop for the night. Once the cloud moved back behind them to protect them from the Egyptians. (Exodus 13:21-22; 14:19-24; 33:8-11; Nehemiah 9:19)

Pisgah, Mount, (PIS-guh) is one of the high spots on Mount Nebo. It was the mountain where Moses stood to see into the promised land. God had earlier spoken to Balaam on Mount Pisgah. (Numbers 23:14-30; Deuteronomy 34:1-4)

plagues (PLAYGZ) is a word sometimes used for certain terrible things that God causes to happen. These are done as a punishment or warning. God sent ten plagues on the land of Egypt. They were to let the Egyptians know that God wanted his people set free. Later, God sent plagues to the Israelites when they started making idols. (Exodus 7–11; 32:35)

plumb line (PLUM LINE) is a string with a rock or other weight on one end. People used it to see if a wall

P

plumb line

was straight. The idea of a plumb line was sometimes used to show that God was checking to see if his people were living right, just as they checked to see if a wall was straight by using a plumb line. (2 Kings 21:13; Amos 7:7-8)

pomegranate (PAHM-gran-it) is a reddish fruit about the size of an apple. It has many seeds. Each seed has a pocket of sweet juice around it. (Exodus 28:33; 39:24; Numbers 13:23; Deuteronomy 8:8; 1 Samuel 14:2)

Potiphar (POT-ih-fur) was an officer for the king of Egypt. He bought Joseph when he was sold as a slave. Potiphar saw that Joseph was very dependable. So, he put Joseph in charge of running his household. Potiphar's wife, however, lied about Joseph and got him into trouble. (Genesis 39)

pottage (POT-edge) is a thick vegetable soup or stew that was eaten in Bible times. It often had beans and meat in it. (Genesis 25:29-34; 2 Kings 4:38-40)

potter (POT-ur) is a person who makes pots and dishes out of clay. He often uses a turning wheel on which to form the clay into the right shape

with his hands. Then it is dried and heated in an oven. Once, God sent Jeremiah the prophet to watch a potter. He showed him that God molds people's lives as a potter molds clay. (Jeremiah 18:1-6; Romans 9:21)

praetorium (pray-TORE-ee-um) was the governor's palace in New Testament times. It was also where Roman soldiers stayed. Court cases were often held here. (Matthew 27:27; John 18:28-33; 19:9; Acts 23:35)

praise (PRAYZ) means to say good things about someone or something. God's people can praise him by singing, praying or by living the way he tells us to live. (Psalms 100; 145; 148; Luke 2:13-14,20; 19:37; Acts 2:47; 3:8-9; Hebrews 2:12)

prayer (PREHR) is talking to God. Jesus prayed often when he was on earth. Sometimes he even prayed all night long. In our prayers we praise God, we thank him for the many good things he does for us, we ask for things we need and we pray for the needs of other people. We should admit our mistakes and ask God to forgive us. (Numbers 21:7; 1 Samuel 1:10-11,27-28; Daniel 6:8-23; Matthew 26:36-44; Luke 6:12,28; 18:1-14; Acts 4:23-41; 7:57-60; James 5:13-18)

Preparation Day (prep-a-RAY-shun DAY) was the day before the Sabbath day. On that day the Jews prepared or got everything ready for the Sabbath. (Luke 23:54; John 19:14,31)

priest (PREEST) in the Old Testament was a servant of God who worked in the Meeting Tent or Temple. Priests helped the people offer their gifts and sacrifices to God. Jesus is the Christian's high priest. He brings man and God together. Because of this all Christians are now priests. (Leviticus 21–22; Hebrews 7:26-28; 1 Peter 2:5,9; Revelation 1:5-6) See "high priest."

Priscilla (prih-SIL-uh) See "Aquila."

prison (PRIH-zun) is a jail where people are locked up as a punishment. In New Testament days many Christians were put in prison because they believed Jesus was the Son of God. Some New Testament books were written from prison cells.

prison

At different times God did miracles to free Peter and Paul from prison. (Acts 5:17-20; 16:23-33; 2 Corinthians 11:23)

procurator (prahk-yur-RATE-ur) See "governor."

prodigal (PRAH-dih-gul) means "careless and wasteful." Jesus told a story about a son who rebelled against his father and wasted all his money doing foolish things. This is often called the story of the prodigal son. He realized his mistake and came home. His father forgave him and celebrated his return. (Luke 15:11-32)

prophecy (PRAH-feh-see) means "message." It is God speaking through chosen people called prophets. The Old Testament has many prophecies about the Savior who was to come into the world. Jesus was the answer to these prophecies. (Ezekiel 12:26-28; 2 Peter 1:20-21; Revelation 22:18-19) See "prophet."

prophesy (PRAH-fes-sy) is to speak a prophecy. See "prophecy."

prophet (PRAH-fet) means "messenger" or one who speaks for someone else. With God's help, a prophet was able to tell the people God's message correctly. Sometimes prophets told what would happen in the future. A woman who spoke God's message was called a prophetess. (2 Kings 22:14; Luke 2:36). Several books of the Old Testament were written by prophets, including Jeremiah, Amos, Jonah and Micah. (2 Kings 6:12-16; 17:12-13; Matthew 2:5-6; Luke 16:29-31; 24:25-27; Romans 1:2; 1 Corinthians 12:28-29; 1 Peter 1:10-12)

prophetess See "prophet."

prostitutes (PRAH-sti-toots) are people who sell their bodies for sex. They have sexual relations with people to whom they are not married. This is a sin. In the Old Testament God's people often worshiped other gods. God said this was acting like a prostitute. (Genesis 38:15; Exodus 34:15-16; Proverbs 23:27; Jeremiah 3:1-6; Hosea 3:3; 1 Corinthians 6:15)

proverbs (PRAH-verbs) are wise sayings. They are usually short so they can be easily remembered. The Old Testament book of Proverbs contains many wise sayings. They tell how to live a good and happy life.

psalm (SAHM) means "song." The book of Psalms is like a song book. The Jews sang many of these psalms, particularly at special times. There are many musical directions in the Psalms, such as the tune or the instruments to be used.

publican (PUB-leh-kun) See "tax collector."

Publius (POOB-lih-us) was the head man of the island of Malta. Paul was shipwrecked there on his way to Rome. Publius helped Paul and his friends. Paul prayed for Publius' sick father, and he got well. (Acts 28:1-10)

Pul See "Tiglath-Pileser."

Purim See "Feast of Purim."

purple is a color that had special meaning in Bible times. Purple clothing was worn by kings, queens and other rich people. The cloth was expensive because the purple dye came from special shellfish. (Mark 15:17; Acts 16:14)

Queen Goddess is another name for Ishtar, a goddess of the Babylonians. During Jeremiah's time some of the Israelites worshiped her. (Jeremiah 7:18; 44:17-25)

Queen of Heaven See "Queen Goddess."

Queen of Sheba (SHE-buh) See "Sheba, Queen of."

Quirinius (kwy-RIN-ee-us) was the

Roman governor of Syria when Jesus was born. He was given this job after he had been a war hero in Asia Minor. (Luke 2:1-3)

quiver (KWIH-vur) is the bag that a bowman wears to hold his arrows. One of the psalms says that having many children is like having a quiver full of arrows because both make a man feel strong and important. Isaiah said that God is like a quiver. The bag keeps arrows safe as God keeps us safe. (Psalm 127:5; Isaiah 49:2; Lamentations 3:13)

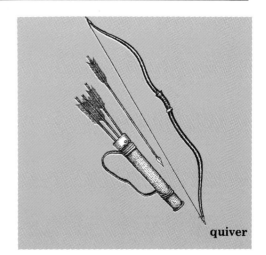

quiver

R

Rabbah (RAB-uh) means "great." Rabbah is the oldest city in the world where people have lived continually. It was the capital city of the Ammonites. Today it is called Amman, Jordan. The city was captured by King David's men. Later, Rabbah and the Ammonites were enemies of the Israelites. Jeremiah said they would be punished for their cruelty. (2 Samuel 11:1; 12:27-29; 17:27; Jeremiah 49:2-3; Amos 1:14)

rabbi (RAB-eye) or **rabboni** (rah-BONE-eye) is a Hebrew word that means "teacher." Jesus' followers often called him this as a sign of respect. (Matthew 23:7-8; John 1:38, 49; 3:2; 4:31)

Rachel (RAY-chel) was a wife of Jacob and the mother of Benjamin and Joseph. Jacob worked for Rachel's father for seven years to be able to marry her. Then Laban, Rachel's father, tricked Jacob into marrying her older sister Leah. So, Jacob worked seven more years for Rachel. Rachel died when Benjamin was born. (Genesis 29–31; 33:1-2; 35:16-20)

Rahab (RAY-hab) was the name of a make-believe dragon. In a well-known story, Rahab looked strong but was defeated. Egypt was sometimes called Rahab to show that it would be defeated as Rahab was. (Job 9:13; 26:12; Psalms 87:4; 89:10; Isaiah 30:7; 51:9)

Rahab was also the name of a

woman in Jericho. She hid the Israelite spies and helped them escape. (Joshua 2:1-3; 6:17-25; Matthew 1:5; Hebrews 11:31; James 2:25)

Rahab

rainbow is a half circle of seven colors in the sky. It is often seen during or after a rain. God gave the rainbow as a sign of his promise not to destroy the whole earth with a flood again. In John's vision of heaven there was a rainbow around God's throne. (Genesis 9:8-17; Revelation 4:3)

Ramah (RAY-muh) is a Hebrew word that means "high." It was the name of several towns that were built on hills:

Ramah, near Bethel, was close to the home of Deborah. This was where Nebuzaradan let Jeremiah go free. It was about five miles north of Jerusalem. Rachel was buried near Ramah. (Judges 4:5; 1 Kings 15:17-22; Jeremiah 31:15; 40:1; Matthew 2:18)

Ramah, the home of Samuel, was where Samuel first met Saul. David once came to Ramah when he was running away from Saul. Some think this Ramah may be the same as the place called Arimathea in the New Testament. (1 Samuel 1:19; 7:17; 19:18)

Rameses (RAM-eh-seez) was one of the cities built by the Israelites when they were slaves in Egypt. The city was a place for storing things. It was named for a king of Egypt. It was from Rameses that the Israelites started out of Egypt on their way to the promised land. (Exodus 1:11; 12:37; Numbers 33:3)

Ramoth Gilead (RAY-moth GIL-ee-ad) was one of the cities of safety on the east side of the Jordan River. It was also a strong, walled city that was involved in many battles. Sometimes it was called Ramoth for short. (Joshua 20:8; 1 Kings 4:13; 2 Kings 8:28; 9:1-14)

Rapha (RAY-fa) was a leader of a group of people in Canaan. They may have been giants. The descendants of Rapha are called Rephaites. (Genesis 14:5; Deuteronomy 2:11; 2 Samuel 21:16-22)

raven is a large bird similar to a crow. It is purplish-black and eats dead things. After the flood, Noah sent out a raven to see if the earth was dry. God used ravens to take care of Elijah when there was little food.

raven

Ravens brought him meat and bread twice a day. (Genesis 8:7; 1 Kings 17:4-6; Isaiah 34:11)

Rebekah (ree-BEK-uh) was the wife of Isaac and the mother of Jacob and Esau. Abraham sent a servant to Haran to find a wife for Isaac among their relatives. The servant asked God to help him find the best wife for Isaac. Read Genesis 24 to see how the Lord did it. Later, when Isaac was old, Rebekah and Jacob tricked him. This caused problems between the sons. Jacob and Esau later made up. (Genesis 24:1-67; 25:19-26; 27:1-46)

reconciliation (REK-on-sil-ee-AY-shun) means bringing people who have been separated back together. Sin separates people from God. Jesus died to reconcile us or make us friends with God again. (Romans 5:6-11; 2 Corinthians 5:18-21; Ephesians 2:12-16; Colossians 1:20-22)

Red Sea is sometimes called the Sea of Reeds. It is a large body of water between Africa and Arabia. At the northern end it has two parts, one on each side of the Sinai Peninsula. God used a miracle to divide these waters on the northern end on the west side. Then the Israelites walked across on dry land and escaped from Egypt. (Exodus 13:17–15:22; Joshua 2:10; 4:23; Psalm 106:7-22) See map.

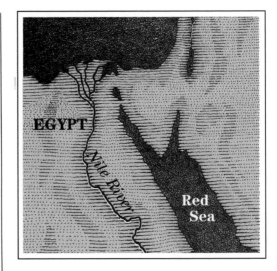

redeem (ree-DEEM) means to buy something back or pay the price to set a slave free. Being a sinner is like being a slave to the devil. Jesus died to buy us back—to set us free—from the devil. The price that was paid was Jesus' blood. (1 Corinthians 6:20; Galatians 4:5; Titus 2:14)

Rehoboam (ree-ho-BO-um) was the son of Solomon and took his place as king. But he was not as wise as his father. He listened to the advice of the wrong people. This caused the ten northern tribes of Israel to leave his kingdom and form the separate country of Israel. He fought with Egypt and Jeroboam, king of Israel. (1 Kings 11:43–14:31; 2 Chronicles 9:31–12:16)

rejoice means to feel great happiness and joy. (Nehemiah 12:43; Luke 19:37; Acts 8:39; Philippians 4:4; 1 Peter 4:13)

remission (rih-MISH-un) See "forgiveness."

remnant (REM-nant) means a small part that is left. In the Bible it usually meant the few Jews who were left alive after their captivity in Babylon. These few people got to return to Jerusalem. (Ezra 9:8; Isaiah 10:20-22; 11:11-16; 37:31)

repent (ree-PENT) means being sorry for doing something wrong and not continuing to do that wrong thing. To repent is to "change your heart and life." (2 Chronicles 32:26; Matthew 3:2; 4:17; Mark 1:15; Luke 15:7,10; Acts 2:38; 3:19)

Rephaites See "Rapha."

resurrection (REZ-uh-REK-shun) is a dead person's coming back to life. In the New Testament several people came back to life with God's help. Some of them were Lazarus (John 11:38-45), Tabitha (Acts 9:36-42), the widow's son in the town of Nain (Luke 7:11-17), and Eutychus (Acts 20:8-12). Jesus, the Son of God, came back to life after being dead three days. This was the most important resurrection. His resurrection from death means we can be saved and live in heaven forever. (Matthew 28:1-10; 1 Corinthians 15; 1 Peter 3:21-22)

Reuben (ROO-ben) was the oldest of Jacob's 12 sons. He saved Joseph's life when the other brothers wanted to kill him. Reuben convinced them to sell Joseph as a slave instead. His descendants were the tribe of Reuben. (Genesis 37:18-30; 46:8-9; Exodus 6:14; Joshua 13:15-23)

revelation (rev-uh-LAY-shun) means to show plainly something that has been hidden. The last book in the New Testament is called the Revelation to John. God showed the apostle John what to write to Christians to give them hope and faith even though they were being persecuted. (2 Corinthians 12:1; Revelation 1:1-3)

Rhoda (ROAD-uh) was a servant girl in the home of John Mark's mother. A group of Christians met there to pray for Peter who was in prison. When someone knocked on the door, Rhoda went to answer. It was Peter! An angel had let him out of prison. She was so excited she forgot to do something. Read the story to see what she forgot to do. (Acts 12:12-17)

righteousness (RY-chuss-ness) means being right with God and doing what is right. No one always does what is right. So we can never be completely righteous. But Jesus is, and he died to share his rightness with us. (Proverbs 10:2; Matthew 3:15; Romans 3:19-26; 4:3; 2 Corinthians 5:21; 6:4-7; Philippians 3:8-9)

Rock is often used as a name for God. A large rock is strong and a good place to hide. God is strong and protects us from our enemies. (Genesis 49:24; Deuteronomy 32:4,15,18,30; 2 Samuel 22:32,47; Psalm 18:2,31,46)

rock badger (ROK BAD-jur), sometimes called a "coney," is known as "the hider" because it hides among

the mountain gorges and rocky areas of Arabia. It is about the size and color of a rabbit, but it has no tail. (Proverbs 30:26; Psalm 104:18)

Romans, letter to the, was written by Paul about A.D. 57 to the church at Rome. He had never been there, but he knew many of the people there and was hoping to go there. The letter to the Romans was Paul's way of letting them know what he preached. It lets us know how God makes us right with him. The last few chapters of Romans tell how a person should live to be right with God.

Rome was the capital city of the Roman Empire at the time of Christ. More than a million people lived there. The book of Romans is Paul's letter to the Christians in Rome. Both the apostle Paul and the apostle Peter probably died as martyrs in Rome. (Acts 23:11; 28:14-16; Romans 1:7; 2 Timothy 1:16-17)

Ruth (ROOTH) is the heroine of the book of Ruth. She was a Moabite woman who was married to an Israelite. After he died, she moved to Bethlehem with her mother-in-law Naomi. There Ruth met Boaz and married him. She became the great-grandmother of King David and an ancestor of Jesus. (Ruth 1–4)

Sabbath (SAB-uth) means "rest." It was the seventh day of the Jewish week, their day of worship to God. The Jews were not allowed to work on this day. Some Jews became angry with Jesus because he healed people on the Sabbath. They thought this was breaking the Old Testament law of the Sabbath. (Exodus 16:23-30; 20:8-11; Matthew 12:9-14; Luke 6:1-11; Acts 18:4; Colossians 2:16-17)

sackcloth (SAK-cloth) was a type of clothing made from rough cloth. It was usually made from the hair of a black goat. People wore sackcloth to show their sadness. It could be sad-

ness because someone had died or because someone was sorry for his sins. (Genesis 37:34-35; 2 Samuel 3:31; 2 Kings 19:1-2; Nehemiah 9: 1-2; Jonah 3:8; Matthew 11:21)

sacrifice (SAK-rih-fice) means to give something valuable to God. In the Old Testament people gave the best of their animals or crops to the Lord. These sacrifices or offerings were given for several reasons: (1)thanking God for what he had done, (2)showing obedience or (3)showing sorrow for sin. Now we do not offer animal sacrifices. Jesus sacrificed himself for us. We are to live as God wants us to—as living sacrifices to him. (Genesis 4:3-5; 8:20; Psalm 50:7-14; Romans 12:1; Hebrews 9: 6-28; 10:1-18; 13:15)

Sadducees (SAD-you-seez) were a Jewish religious group. They were rich and important men. They believed that only the first five books of the Old Testament were true. They did not believe in angels or life after death (resurrection). The Sadducees lost their power and importance after Jerusalem was destroyed by the Romans about the year A.D. 70. (Matthew 22:23-33; Acts:4:1-2; 5:17-18; 23:6-9)

safety, city of, is sometimes called City of Refuge. In Bible times, someone who had accidentally killed another person could go to a city of safety for protection. As long as the person was in a city of safety, the dead person's relative could not punish him. There were six cities of safety. (Numbers 35:6-34; Joshua 20)

saffron (SAF-ron) is a purple flower. Parts of it are used as a spice. (Song of Solomon 4:14)

saint is another word for Christian.

God has set Christians apart to serve him. They live to please God and be like him—pure and holy. (Acts 9:13,32,41; 26:10; Romans 1:7; 1 Corinthians 1:2; Ephesians 1:1)

Word Clues

salary
is the amount a person is paid for doing his job. It comes from the word "salt." In Bible times salt was very valuable. Soldiers were paid in salt. That's where the phrase came from, "He's worth his salt." Today a person who does a good job gets a "salary" because he is "worth his salt."

Salem (SAY-lem) means "peace." It is an old name for Jerusalem. (Hebrews 7:1-2)

Salome (sah-LO-mee) was the name of two women in the New Testament:

   Salome was the name of the daughter of Herodias and Herod Philip, although the Bible does not call her by name. She once danced for Herod on his birthday. It pleased him so much that he promised her anything she wanted. Her mother had her ask for the head of John

saffron

the Baptist. So, Herod had John's head cut off and brought to her on a platter. (Matthew 14:6-12; Mark 6:17-29)

Salome, the wife of Zebedee, was the mother of the apostles James and John. She was also probably a sister to Mary, the mother of Jesus. She was present at Jesus' death on the cross. She also saw him after he came back to life. (Mark 15:40; 16:1)

salt was important in Bible times because it preserved food and improved its flavor. It was sprinkled on sacrifices in the Temple. When two people made an agreement, they would eat some salt as a sign that they would keep their promises. (Leviticus 2:13; Matthew 5:13)

Salt Sea See "Dead Sea."

salvation (sal-VAY-shun) means being rescued from some kind of danger. Sometimes the Bible talks about being saved or rescued from injury or death. For example, God rescued the Israelites from the Egyptians when he divided the Red Sea and let the Israelites cross on dry land. This kept the Egyptians from capturing or killing them.

But salvation usually means being rescued or saved from sin and its punishment. Jesus came to save us from sin and the death it causes. (Exodus 14:13; 2 Samuel 22:1-7; Luke 19:9; Romans 1:16; 1 Corinthians 1:18; Ephesians 1:13; Philippians 2:12; Hebrews 1:14)

Samaritan (sah-MEHR-ih-t'n) was a person from the area of Samaria in Palestine. Samaria was between Galilee and Judea. These people were only part Jewish, so the Jews did not accept them. They hated the Samaritans. But Jesus showed love and concern for the Samaritans. One story that Jesus told is known as the story of "the good Samaritan." (Luke 10:30-37; John 4:1-42)

Samson (SAM-son) was one of Israel's judges. He was famous for his great strength. An angel told his parents about his special strength before he was born. Samson helped the Israelites fight against their enemy the Philistines. But he broke his special promise to God and was captured by the Philistines. He died by pulling down a huge building on top of many Philistines and himself. (Judges 13–16) See also "Manoah" and "Delilah."

Samuel (SAM-u-el) was the last judge in Israel. God used him to appoint both Saul and David as kings. (1 Samuel 1–3; 7–16)

Samuel, books of, (SAM-u-el) were first written as one book. They were divided into two books about 200 B.C. when the Old Testament was being translated into the Greek language. They are named for Samuel the prophet, but we do not really know who wrote them. First Samuel tells about the last judge and the first king of Israel, Saul. Second Samuel covers the years David was king.

Sanballat (san-BAL-lat) was governor of Samaria when the Israelites were rebuilding the walls of Jerusalem. He did not want them to do it. Sanballat tried several ways to prevent them from finishing the job. But Nehemiah was such a good

S

leader that Sanballat was not able to stop them. (Nehemiah 4–6)

sanctify (SANK-teh-fy) means to "make holy" or "make ready for service." God and his Spirit set Christians apart to serve him. God's Spirit continues helping us become more and more like Jesus. This is called "sanctification." (Romans 6:19-22; 1 Thessalonians 5:23; Hebrews 13:12; 1 Peter 1:2)

sanctuary (SANK-choo-air-ee) See "Holy Place."

Sanhedrin (san-HEE-drin) See "council."

Sapphira (sah-FY-ruh) was the wife of Ananias. She and her husband lied about what they were giving to the Lord. Read the story of what happened to them in Acts 5:1-11.

Sarah (SAIR-uh) was the wife of Abraham. At first her name was Sarai, but the Lord changed it. She had no children until she was 90 years old. Then she heard an angel tell Abraham that she would have a child. She didn't believe it and laughed. But the next year their son Isaac was born. (Genesis 11–12; 16–18; 20–21)

Satan (SAY-t'n) in Hebrew means "enemy." It is a name for the devil, the enemy of God and man. (1 Chronicles 21:1; Job 1:6-9; Matthew 4:10; Luke 10:18-19; Acts 5:3; 26:18) See "devil."

Saul (SAWL) in the Old Testament was the first king of Israel (1 Samuel 9–31). Saul in the New Testament was a man whose name was changed to Paul. See "Paul."

savior (SAVE-yor) is someone who saves people from danger. The name Jesus means "savior." Jesus is the Savior of the people of this world. His life, death and resurrection made it possible for people to be saved from death and punishment for their sins. (Luke 2:11; John 4:42; Ephesians 5:23; Philippians 3:20; Titus 1:4; 1 John 4:14)

scarlet (SCAR-let) means a bright red color. Some of the cloth in the Meeting Tent and the priests' clothes were this color. (Exodus 26:1,31,36; 28:5-8,15,33; Joshua 2:17)

scepter (SEP-tur) is a wand or a rod that the king holds. It is a sign of his power. Some are long and thin.

scepter

Others are short and flat like a paddle. Some of them are highly decorated with gold. (Esther 4:11; 5:2; 8:4; Psalm 2:9)

scourge (SKURJ) means to beat someone with a whip or stick. This was done as punishment. The Jews were only allowed to strike a person 40 times. They usually stopped at 39 to be sure they didn't break the rule. The Romans could scourge people for several reasons. But they couldn't scourge a Roman citizen. Sometimes

scourge

the whip had pieces of bone or metal in the end of the leather strips. Jesus was beaten with this kind of whip. (Mark 10:34; 15:15; Acts 22:24-29; Hebrews 11:36)

scribe is a Hebrew word that means to write, to count and to put in order. In New Testament times scribes were men who wrote copies of the Scriptures. They were very careful when they copied the words of God. To be sure they had not made a mistake in copying, they would count the number of letters on each line they wrote. Scribes were educated, and some of them served as secretaries, royal assistants and teachers. (Nehemiah 8:1; Jeremiah 36:26; Matthew 7:29; 15:1-9; 23:1-36; Luke 22:2)

Scriptures (SCRIP-churs) means "writings." They are the special writings of God's word for man. When the word Scriptures is used in the New Testament, it usually means the Old Testament. Later, it came to mean the whole Bible. (Daniel 9:2; Luke 24:27,32,45; Acts 8:32-35; 17:2,11; 2 Timothy 3:16; 2 Peter 1:20; 3:16) See "Bible."

scroll is a long roll of paper used for writing. In Bible times books were written on scrolls. These scrolls were rolled up from each end to the middle. They were made of papyrus (a plant) or parchment (an animal

scroll

skin). Some scrolls were as long as 35 feet. (Numbers 5:23; Isaiah 8:1; Jeremiah 36; Luke 4:17-20; 2 Timothy 4:13; Revelation 5:1-5)

Scythians (SITH-ee-unz) were a group of wandering people who lived near the Black Sea. They were known for being wild and cruel. (Colossians 3:11)

Sea of Galilee See "Galilee, Lake."

Sea of Reeds See "Red Sea."

seal was a tool with a design or picture carved on it. Kings pressed this

S

seal into wax which had been melted onto important papers to close them. It was like a person's signature. If the seal was broken, it showed that someone else had looked at the papers. A seal also showed who owned something. Sometimes these seals were worn as rings. (1 Kings 21:8; Esther 8:8; 2 Corinthians 1:22) See "signet ring."

second coming of Christ is the time when Jesus will return. Jesus went back to heaven in a cloud. The angels said, "He will come back in the same way you saw him go." In 1 Thessalonians Paul tells us that God's people who are dead will meet those who are alive in the air. So "we will be with the Lord forever." Only God knows exactly when this will happen, but Jesus has promised to come back. (John 14:3; Acts 1:11; 1 Thessalonians 4:16-17; Titus 2:11-14; Hebrews 9:28; 2 Peter 3)

seer was another name for prophet. (1 Samuel 9:9) See "prophet."

Selah (SEE-lah) is probably a musical direction and is used in the Psalms. It may mean to pause. The word was not intended to be spoken when reading the Psalm. (Psalms 3; 4; 9; 24)

Sennacherib (sen-AK-ur-ib) was king of Assyria from 705-681 B.C. He captured a large area of the Bible lands. His huge army surrounded Jerusalem. But one night an angel killed thousands of Assyrians. So, Sennacherib and his remaining soldiers went back to Nineveh. Later, he was murdered by his own sons. (2 Kings 18–19; Isaiah 36–37)

Sermon on the Mount is a sermon Jesus preached as he was sitting on the side of a mountain near Lake Galilee. Jesus described the difference God's kingdom makes in a person's life. This sermon contains the famous "beatitudes." (Matthew 5–7)

serpent See "snake."

Seth was the third son of Adam and Eve. He was born after Abel died. He died at age 912. (Genesis 4: 25-26)

Shadrach (SHAYD-rak), **Meshach** (ME-shak) and **Abednego** (ah-BED-nee-go) were the Babylonian names given to three Hebrew boys—Hananiah, Mishal and Azariah. They were friends of Daniel. They all had been taken as captives to Babylon. They refused to bow down and worship a false god. For this they were put in a blazing furnace. Read the surprise ending to the story in Daniel 3:21-30. (Daniel 1; 3)

Shallum (SHAL-um) was the name of several people in the Old Testament. Here are two of them:

Shallum, King of Israel, ruled for only one month in 752 B.C. (2 Kings 15:10-15)

Shallum, King of Judah, was usually called Jehoahaz. He was the son of Josiah. (2 Kings 23:30-34)

Shalmaneser (shal-mah-NEE-zer) was the name of several kings of Assyria. One of them is mentioned in the Bible. Shalmaneser the fifth attacked Israel and put Hoshea, the last king of Israel, in prison. (2 Kings 17)

Shaphan (SHAY-fan) was an assistant to King Josiah. He helped make sure the Temple was repaired. When the Book of the Teachings was found there, he read it. Then he took it and read some to King Josiah. When Josiah heard Shaphan read from the book, he was upset. Read the story to find out why. (2 Kings 22:3-13)

sharing means giving something of yours to someone else. It also means to enjoy something together with others. In New Testament times Christians sold their houses or land and gave the money to help other Christians. (Acts 2:42-47; 4:32; 1 Corinthians 1:9; 2 Corinthians 8:4) See "fellowship."

Sharon (SHAIR-un) is the name of the plain along the coast of the Mediterranean Sea. It runs from Joppa to Mount Carmel. (1 Chronicles 27:29; Song of Solomon 2:1; Isaiah 33:9; 65:10)

sheaf (SHEEF) is a bundle of grain stalks that have been cut and tied

sheaf

together. (Genesis 37:7; Leviticus 23:10; Job 24:10)

Sheba, Queen of, (SHE-buh) came to visit Solomon. Her land was in southwest Arabia. She had heard about how rich and wise he was. But she wanted to see for herself. So, she rode camels for over 1,000 miles. After her visit, the queen said, "Your wisdom and wealth are much greater than I had heard." (1 Kings 10:1-13)

Shebna (SHEB-nuh) was the manager of the palace for King Hezekiah. He took messages from Hezekiah to the king of Assyria. The prophet Isaiah criticized Shebna for building such an expensive tomb for himself. (2 Kings 18:18–19:6; Isaiah 22:15-21)

sheep are tame animals raised for their wool, meat and skins. They were very important to the Jews because the sheep gave the people clothes, food and skins for their tents. In the New Testament, Christians are called sheep and Jesus is called the "Good Shepherd." That

means that Christians follow Jesus and let him guide them through life. (1 Samuel 17:15-35; Luke 15:1-7; John 10:1-30; 21:15-17; 1 Peter 2:25) See "shepherd."

Shem was Noah's oldest son. His descendants became the Jews and the other nations in that area of the world. (Genesis 6:10; 10:21-31)

sheminith (SHEM-ih-nith) means "on the eighth." It is probably a musical word in the Psalms that means an octave (eight notes). It may mean

S

to use an instrument with eight strings. (1 Chronicles 15:21; Psalms 6; 12)

sheol (SHEE-ole) is the Hebrew word for the place where dead people are. (Job 17:13-16; Psalm 139:8; Luke 16:23-26)

shepherd (SHEP-'rd) is a person who cares for and protects sheep. A shepherd loves his sheep and gives them food and water. He guides them to a quiet place to rest. He protects the sheep from wolves and other wild animals. A good shepherd will even die trying to protect his sheep.

Jesus is called the Good Shepherd because he loves and cares for his followers who are often called sheep. Jesus was willing to die for his followers to save them. (Psalm 23; Mark 6:34; John 10:1-30; 1 Peter 2:25; 5:4)

Sheshbazzar (shesh-BAZ-ur) was governor of the Jews in 538 B.C. This was when Cyrus, King of Persia, let the Jews go back to rebuild the Temple. Sheshbazzar brought back the valuable bowls and pans. These had been taken from the Temple. He helped the people start rebuilding the Temple. (Ezra 1:7-11; 5:13-17)

shiggaion (shi-GY-on) is probably a musical word used in the Psalms. It may mean that the Psalm is a sad song. (Psalm 7)

Shiloh (SHY-lo) was a town in the hill country north of Jerusalem. This was one of Joshua's headquarters when the Israelites were capturing the promised land. The Meeting Tent was kept there during the time of the judges. So it was a kind of spiritual capital city. (Joshua 18: 1,8; Judges 18:31)

Shimei (SHIM-ee-i) was a relative of King Saul. When Absalom rebelled against King David, Shimei cursed David. Later he apologized to David. (2 Samuel 16:5-14; 19:16-23; 1 Kings 2:36-46)

ships were not very important to the Jews. They were afraid of the oceans and didn't travel there much. Jews did fish on Lake Galilee. Solomon owned many ships and sent them to buy and sell in far away places. In the New Testament Paul often traveled on a ship and seemed to know a lot about sea travel. (1 Kings 9: 26-28; 22:48-49; Luke 5:3; Acts 27; 2 Corinthians 11:25)

Shishak (SHY-shak) was king of Egypt during the time of Solomon and Rehoboam. He attacked both Israel and Judah when Jeroboam and Rehoboam were the kings. Shishak captured several cities and stole treasures from the Temple. (1 Kings 11:40; 14:25-28; 2 Chronicles 12:1-9)

showbread See "bread that shows we are in God's presence."

Shunamite (SHOO-nah-mite) was a person from Shunem. This was a town in northern Israel. A wealthy woman there built a room on her house for Elisha. Elisha helped her more than once. (2 Kings 4:8-37; 8:1-6)

sickle (SICK-ul) was a tool for cutting grain. In early Bible times it was made of flint rock in a curved wooden frame. Later, sickles were made of metal with a wooden handle. They

sickle

looked like a large knife with a curved blade. (Revelation 14:14-19)

Sidon (SY-don) was a Phoenician city on the coast of the Mediterranean Sea. It is part of the nation of Lebanon today. Jezebel was the daughter of the king of Sidon. Baal and Ashtoreth were the false gods of Sidon. (1 Kings 16:31; Isaiah 23:1-2; Mark 7:31; Acts 27:3)

siege mound (SEEJ) was dirt piled against a city wall to make it easier for attackers to climb up and shoot arrows into the city. It was also used to help the attackers climb over the wall into the city. (2 Samuel 20:15; Isaiah 37:33; Jeremiah 6:6)

signet ring (SIG-net ring) was a ring worn by a king or other important

person. It had his seal on it. He would stamp things with this ring

to show that he owned them. The stamp was like a signature. (Genesis 41:42; Esther 3:10; 8:2-10; Daniel 6:17) See "seal."

Sihon (SY-hon) was a king of the Amorites when the Israelites came out of Egypt. They asked for permission to go through the Amorites' land. But Sihon would not allow it. He came out to fight them instead. In the battle Sihon was killed and the Israelites won. (Numbers 21: 21-31; Deuteronomy 3:1-8; Judges 11:12-28)

Silas (SY-lus) is sometimes called Silvanus. He was a teacher in the church in Jerusalem who often traveled with Paul. He became one of Paul's most trusted helpers. He may have written down some of Peter's and Paul's letters for them. (Acts 15:22,30–17:16; 18:5; 1 Thessalonians 1:1; 1 Peter 5:12)

Siloam, Pool of, (sy-LO-um) was a pool of water in the city of Jerusalem. It is sometimes called the "pool between two walls." The water in the pool flowed in from a spring outside the city walls. Jesus healed a man who was born blind by having him wash in the Pool of Siloam. (John 9:7-12)

Silvanus (sil-VAY-nus) See "Silas."

Simeon (SIM-ee-un) is a name that means "God has heard." He was 1 of the 12 sons of Israel. (Genesis 29:33; 35:23)

Another Simeon was a godly man who lived in Jerusalem. When he saw the baby Jesus in the Temple, he knew that this child would save his people from their sins. He held the baby Jesus in his arms and said a prayer of thanks to God. (Luke 2:25-35)

Simon (SY-mun), sometimes called Simeon, is a name that means "God has heard." The apostle Peter was first named Simon. Other men named Simon are also mentioned in the New Testament:

Simon, the brother of Jesus (Matthew 13:55)

Simon of Cyrene carried the cross of Jesus to the hill of Calvary. (Matthew 27:32)

Simon, the magician, tried to buy the power of the Holy Spirit to do miracles. (Acts 8:9-24)

Simon, the Zealot, was 1 of the 12 apostles. (Matthew 10:4)

sin is a word, thought or act against the law of God. Sin is doing something God said not to do, or it could be not doing something he said to do. Jesus came to save us from being punished for our sins. (Psalm 32:2; Romans 3:23; 5:12; 1 Corinthians 15:3; Galatians 1:4; Hebrews 4:15-16; 1 John 1:8-10; 2:1-2)

Sinai (SY-ny) is a mountain in the desert between Egypt and Canaan. The Israelites were camped there when God gave Moses the Ten Commandments. This was also where Elijah ran to get away from Jezebel. The mountain called Jebel Musa today is probably the Mount Sinai in the Bible. (Exodus 19:1-25; 24:16; 1 Kings 19:1-8; Nehemiah 9:13)

singing is a way of praising God and teaching each other. (Matthew 26:30; Acts 16:25; Ephesians 5:19; Colossians 3:16)

Sisera (SIS-er-uh) was captain of a Canaanite army. The Canaanites were enemies of the Israelites and caused them much trouble. But with Deborah and Barak leading, the Israelites defeated Sisera's army. Sisera escaped and hid in a woman's tent. While he slept, she killed him. (Judges 4)

Word Clues

skin of my teeth means to barely escape alive. "He got away by the skin of his teeth." It comes from Job 19:20 where Job describes the terrible things that have happened to him.

slave was a servant owned by someone. The master could do whatever he wanted with the slave. Many slaves and masters became Christians. As the Good News about Jesus spread, slavery began to disappear in the Roman Empire. One famous slave in the New Testament was Onesimus. See "Onesimus." Christians are to be slaves to Christ. He is to be their master. (Deuteronomy 21:14; Romans 6:18; Ephesians 6:5-9; Philemon)

slave woman or "concubine" belonged to a king or other rich family. She had children like a wife, but she was not considered equal to a wife. Later this practice stopped. (Genesis 21:10; 22:24; Exodus 21:7,10)

sling was a weapon for throwing rocks. It was made of two narrow strips of leather that were tied to a larger piece in the middle. The larger piece of leather was wrapped around the rock. The person tied one of the narrow strips around his wrist. He held the end of the other strip in his hand. Then after swing-

sling

ing it around several times, he let go of the loose end. The rock would fly out at great speed. Since the rocks often weighed from two to four pounds each, the sling could be a deadly weapon. (Judges 20:16; 1 Samuel 17:40-50; 1 Chronicles 12:2)

slothful (SLAWTH-ful) means lazy and undependable. (Proverbs 6:6-11; 12:24,27; 13:4; 19:15)

sluggard See "slothful."

snake in the Bible usually means a poisonous snake. Satan appeared as a snake in the garden of Eden. (Genesis 3:1-14; Exodus 7:10; Acts 28:3)

Sodom (SOD-um) was a town known for its evil people. God destroyed it because not even ten good people could be found there. Today, the southern end of the Dead Sea probably covers the area where Sodom was. (Genesis 18:17–19:29; Matthew 10:15)

Solomon (SOL-o-mon) was a son of David. He took his father's place as king. He was famous for his wisdom and for building the Temple in Jeru-salem. (1 Kings 1–11; 2 Chronicles 1–11)

Solomon's Porch (SOL-o-mon's PORCH) was a covered courtyard on the east side of the Temple. People gathered there to sell animals and exchange money. Others met to discuss the Law of Moses. (1 Kings 7:6; John 10:23; Acts 3:11; 5:12)

Son of David was a name the Jews used for the Christ who was to save the world. This was because the Savior was to come from the family of King David. Jesus was the "Son of David." (Matthew 9:27; 20:30; 21:9)

Son of Man was a name Jesus called himself. It showed that he was God's Son, but he was also a man. This title for Jesus comes from "one who looked like a human being" in Daniel 7:13-14. There Daniel prophesies about Jesus. (Matthew 24:30; 26:64; Mark 13:26; 14:62; Luke 21:27; 22:69)

Song of Solomon is an Old Testament book that is sometimes called the Song of Songs. It was probably written by Solomon. It is a group of love poems. It shows how beautiful the love between a man and woman can be.

sons of the prophets were a group of young prophets who learned from an older prophet. They were not his actual children but more like students. (1 Samuel 19:19-20; 2 Kings 2:3-5) See also "prophet."

sorcery (SOR-sir-ee) means trying to put magical spells on people or harming them by some kind of magic. The Bible warns against doing this. (Leviticus 19:26; Deuteronomy 18:14; 2 Kings 17:17)

S

soul (SOLE) is what makes a person alive. Sometimes the Bible writers used words like "heart" and "soul" to mean a person's whole being or the person himself. (Deuteronomy 4:29; Psalm 108:1; Matthew 10:28)

southern kingdom is a name for the two tribes of Israel who did not rebel against Rehoboam. The two tribes were Judah and Benjamin. This nation was often just called Judah. The ten northern tribes that followed Jeroboam were called Israel. (1 Kings 12)

sower was someone who planted seeds so they would grow into crops. He usually walked through the field with a bag of seeds, scattering them as he went. (Matthew 13; Mark 4) See also "farmer's year."

Spirit See "Holy Spirit."

spirit (SPIH-rit) is the part of man that was made to be like God because God is spirit. The New Testament also talks about evil spirits. (Isaiah 26:9; John 4:23-24; James 2:24-26) See "demons," "Holy Spirit" and "soul."

spiritual gifts are the special talents or abilities that God gives to his people. These talents are to help us serve each other and help the church to grow. (Romans 12:6-8; 1 Corinthians 12:1-11; 14:1-25; Ephesians 4:7-13)

spring is a natural fountain where water comes out of the ground. Springs often provide drinking water. (James 3:12; 2 Peter 2:17)

staff was the name for a shepherd's walking stick. It was used to guide and protect the sheep. A shepherd also needed a staff when walking or

climbing in rugged areas. Sometimes a shepherd's staff had a crook at the top which he could use to lift or guide a sheep. (Psalm 23:4; Matthew 10:10; Hebrews 11:21)

Stephen (STEE-ven) was one of the seven men chosen to serve the church in Jerusalem. The New Testament says he was a man who had much faith. He was able to do miracles. Stephen was the first martyr for Christ. The Jews killed him by throwing stones at him because he taught that Jesus was the Son of God. (Acts 6:5-15; 7:54-60; 22:20)

stoning was a Hebrew way of killing criminals. Rocks were thrown at the person until he died. There had to be at least two or three witnesses who agreed that the person had committed a crime. The witnesses threw the first stones. (Deuteronomy 17: 2-7; 1 Kings 21:13; Acts 7:58-60; 14: 5-7)

strong drink is an alcoholic drink like wine or beer. (Deuteronomy 29:6; Proverbs 20:1; 31:4-6; Isaiah 5:11)

swaddling cloths are the pieces of cloth that were wrapped around a

newborn baby in Jesus' time. (Luke 2:7-12)

Sychar (SY-kar) is a small town in Samaria near Jacob's well. Jesus met and taught a woman there. Be-cause of her, many of the people in Sychar believed in Jesus. (John 4)

synagogue (SIN-uh-gog) is a Greek word that means "a meeting." By the first century, the Jews met in synagogues to read and study the Scriptures. The building was also used as the Jewish court and as a school. Both Jesus and Paul often went to the Jewish synagogues to teach and discuss the Scriptures. (Matthew 4:23; Luke 4:16-17; Acts 15:21; 17:1,10)

Syria (SEER-ee-uh) is a Hebrew word that means "plain." In New Testament times it was the area north of Galilee and east of the Mediterranean Sea. Damascus was its capital city. In Old Testament times, this country was called Aram. (1 Kings 11:25; 2 Kings 5:1; Matthew 4:24; 15:23) See "Aram."

T

tabernacle (TAB-er-NAK-'l) See "Meeting Tent."

tablets of the agreement, or tablets of the covenant, were the two flat stones on which God wrote the Ten Commandments. Moses broke the first set. He was coming back down the mountain when he saw that the Israelites had made an idol. He was so upset, he threw the tablets to the ground. Later, he cut two new flat stones. God rewrote the commandments on the new ones. These were kept in the Holy Box inside the Meeting Tent and the Temple. (Exodus 24:12-18; 32:15-16; 34:1-4; Deuteronomy 9:9-17; 10:1-10; 1 Kings 8:9; Hebrews 9:4)

Tabor, Mount, (TAY-bur) is in the Valley of Jezreel about 12 miles from Lake Galilee. This is where Barak gathered his army to attack Sisera.

Early Christians thought this was where Jesus' transfiguration took place. (Joshua 19:22; Judges 4:6-14; Psalm 89:12)

tambourine (tam-bah-REEN) is a musical instrument that is beaten to

keep rhythm. (Exodus 15:20; 1 Samuel 18:6; Psalm 81:2)

Tarshish (TAR-shish) was a city somewhere on the western side of the Mediterranean Sea. It may have been in Spain. This was where Jonah tried to go when God told him to go to Nineveh. (Jonah 1:3; 4:2) See "Jonah."

Tarsus (TAR-sus) was the most important city in Cilicia, which is now the country of Turkey. Tarsus was known as a great place of learning. The apostle Paul was from Tarsus. (Acts 9:11,30; 11:25-26; 21:39; 22:3)

tax collector was a Jew hired by the Romans to collect taxes. Most people did not like tax collectors because they worked for the Romans and often cheated people. The apostle Matthew was a tax collector before he became an apostle. Zacchaeus was also a tax collector. (Matthew 9:10-11; 10:3; Luke 5:27; 19:1-8)

temple (TEM-p'l) is a building where people worship their gods. God told the Jewish people to worship him at the Temple in Jerusalem. This Temple had been built by King Solomon. It was later destroyed by the Babylonians. It was rebuilt by Zerubbabel. This Temple was probably destroyed by a Roman general, Pompey. Herod built a third Temple which was used in Jesus' time. (2 Chronicles 2–7; Ezra 3:10-12; Mark 11:15-17; Acts 7:47; 19:27)

The New Testament also speaks of a Christian's body as a temple. That is because God's Spirit lives in the Christian. (Acts 7:48; 19:27; 1 Corinthians 6:19)

temptation (temp-TAY-shun) is the devil's trying to get us to do something wrong. God has promised to help us when we are tempted, so we can choose to do the right thing. (Matthew 4:1-11; 1 Corinthians 10:13; Hebrews 2:18; 4:15-16; James 1:12-14)

Ten Commandments is a name for the ten rules God gave Moses on Mount Sinai. They were written on two flat stones. The first four rules are about how a person acts toward God. The other six tell how people should treat each other. (Exodus 20:2-20; Deuteronomy 5)

Tent See "Meeting Tent."

testament (TES-tah-ment) See "agreement."

Thaddaeus (THAD-ee-us) was 1 of the 12 apostles. Little else is known about him. (Matthew 10:3; Mark 3:18)

Theophilus (thee-AHF-ih-lus) is a name meaning "friend of God." Luke wrote the books of Luke and Acts to Theophilus. He probably had an important job in the Roman government. (Luke 1:1-3; Acts 1:1)

Thessalonians, letters to, (thes-uh-LONE-ee-unz) are two of the books in the New Testament. Paul wrote them to the church in Thessalonica. In the first letter he reminded them that Jesus was coming back. This means that Christians should be ready for him by living good lives.

Paul's second letter cleared up some mistaken ideas they had gotten from the first letter. Some people were so interested in Jesus' return, they quit working. In 2 Thessalonians Paul made it clear that everyone should work for his food.

Thessalonica (THES-ah-lah-NY-kah) was the capital of the country of Macedonia, which is now northern Greece. It was named after the sister of Alexander the Great. It was important because it was on the famous Egnatian (eg-NAY-shun) Highway. Paul, along with Silas and Timothy, began a church there on his second missionary journey. He wrote 1 and 2 Thessalonians as letters to the Christians in this city. It is still an important city in Greece today. (Acts 17:1-9; 1 Thessalonians 1:1; 2 Thessalonians 1:1)

Thomas (TOM-us), or Didymus, is a name that means "twin." He was 1 of Jesus' 12 apostles. His courage and love for Jesus are shown in John 11:16. Sometimes people call him "doubting Thomas." The other apostles told him Jesus had been raised from death. But Thomas did not believe it until he saw Jesus himself. (John 14:5-7; 20:24-29; 21:2)

threshing floor was a place where farmers separated grain from chaff.

This was done by beating the stalks on the hard ground. Then they would throw it in the air and let the wind blow the chaff away. (Genesis 50:10; Judges 6:11; 2 Samuel 24:16-24) See "chaff."

throne is a special chair for a king. The throne shows his powerful position. The New Testament says Jesus is on a throne in heaven. There he reigns as King of kings. (1 Kings 10:18-19; Matthew 5:34; 19:28-30; Hebrews 4:16; Revelation 3:21)

Thummim (THUM-im) The Urim and Thummim were something attached to the holy vest of the high priest. They may have been gems. They were used in some way to find out what God wanted the Israelites to do. (Exodus 28:30; Leviticus 8:8; Deuteronomy 33:8)

Thyatira (THY-ah-TY-rah) was an important city in Asia. It was famous for the purple cloth that was made there. It is now called Akhisor, Turkey. Lydia, the first Christian on the European continent, was from Thyatira. One of the seven letters written by the apostle John in the book of Revelation was to the Christians there. (Acts 16:14-15; Revelation 1:11; 2:18-29)

Tiberius Caesar (tie-BEER-ee-us SEE-zur) was the Roman emperor during the last half of Jesus' life. He ruled from A.D. 14 to 37. The city of Tiberias was named for him. (Luke 3:1)

Tiglath-Pileser (TIG-lath peh-LEE-zur) was the king of Assyria. He helped Ahaz, King of Judah, fight against Israel and Syria. Later, Tiglath-Pileser captured Babylon and changed his name to Pul. (2 Kings 15:19-20; 16:7-10; 2 Chronicles 28:20)

Tigris (TY-gris) is a great river in the eastern part of the Bible lands. It begins in the mountains of Turkey and runs into the Persian Gulf. Nineveh and the Garden of Eden were both along the Tigris River. (Genesis 2:14; Daniel 10:4)

Timothy (TIM-oh-thee) means "one who honors God." Timothy was a close friend and helper of the apostle Paul. He was the son of a Greek father and Jewish Christian mother. His mother Eunice and his grandmother Lois taught him the Scriptures. Paul wrote two letters, called 1 and 2 Timothy, to him. (Acts 16:1-3; 17:13-16; 1 Corinthians 4:17; 1 Thessalonians 3:1-6; 2 Timothy 1:2-5)

Timothy, letters to, were Paul's last letters in the New Testament. In 1 Timothy he gives the young preacher, Timothy, instructions on choosing church leaders and how the church should be run. In 2 Timothy Paul expects to be killed soon for being, a Christian. He wants Timothy to come see him before he dies.

tithe (TIETH) means "tenth." In the Old Testament the Jewish people were told to give one-tenth of what they earned to God. (Leviticus 27:30-32; Malachi 3:8; Luke 11:42; 18:12)

Titus (TIE-tus) was a trusted friend and helper of the apostle Paul. He often traveled with or for Paul. Paul wrote the book of Titus to him while Titus was on the island of Crete. (2 Corinthians 2:13; 7:6-7,13-15; 8:6,16,23; Titus 1:4-5)

Tobiah (toe-BY-uh) tried to keep Nehemiah from rebuilding the walls of Jerusalem. We don't know why he was against it. First, Tobiah made fun of the rebuilding. Then, he and Sanballat tried to have Nehemiah killed, but they did not succeed. (Nehemiah 2:10-20; 6:10-19; 13:4-9) See also "Nehemiah" and "Sanballat."

tomb (TOOM) is a place where a dead person's body is buried. Some tombs were underground. More often, in biblical times they were dug out of the side of a huge rock or mountain. A large stone was then rolled in front of the tomb to seal it. (Genesis 50:5; Luke 23:53-55; 24:1-2; John 20:1-9; 11:38-41)

Tower of Babel See "Babel, Tower of."

transfiguration (tranz-fig-you-RAY-shun) means "to change." Jesus was transfigured in front of Peter, James and John. Jesus had taken them up on a mountain with him. There his face and clothes began to shine brightly. God spoke to the apostles. He said that Jesus is his Son and that they should obey only him. (Matthew 17:1-9)

tree of life was a special tree in the center of the garden of Eden. Eating the fruit of that tree must have kept a person from dying. But there was another tree in the garden called the tree of knowledge. Adam and Eve were not supposed to eat from that tree. But they did and had to leave the garden so they could not eat from the tree of life. But in Revelation John saw the tree of life again. It was in heaven near God's throne. There no one will ever die. (Genesis 2:9; 3:22-25; Revelation 22:1-2)

trespass See "sin."

tribe was all the descendants of a certain person. The 12 tribes of Israel were the descendants of the 12 sons of Jacob, who was later named Israel. (Genesis 49:28; Joshua 3:12; 7:14)

trigon (TRY-gahn) was a musical instrument used in Old Testament times. It was a harp or lyre shaped

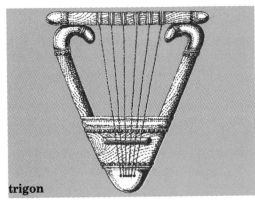

trigon

like a triangle (Daniel 3:5,7,10,15) See also "harp" and "lyre."

triumphal entry (tri-UMF-ul) is the time Jesus entered Jerusalem just before his death on the cross. Crowds of people cheered him as a king. Some people spread their coats on the ground in front of the donkey he was riding. Others used palm branches. They were all shouting praises to God. (Matthew 21:1-11)

Troas (TRO-az) was one of the most important cities in northwest Asia. Its full name was Alexandria Troas. Paul was in Troas when he had a vision of a man asking him to come to the country of Macedonia to help them. He also brought Eutychus back to life in Troas. (Acts 16:8-10; 20:5-12; 2 Corinthians 2:12)

Trophimus (TROF-eh-mus) was a non-Jewish Christian who traveled with Paul. He helped Paul take money to the poor Christians in Jerusalem. (Acts 20:3-6; 21:29-40; 2 Timothy 4:20)

trumpet (TRUM-pet) in Bible times was made from animal horns. It was

trumpet

used to call an army together or announce something important. There were also metal trumpets used for music in the Temple. (Numbers 10: 2-10; Joshua 6:4-20; Judges 3:27; 2 Chronicles 5:12-13; Psalm 81:3; 1 Corinthians 15:52)

tunic (TOO-nik) was a kind of coat. It was a long undergarment similar to a shirt. It draped over one shoulder and down to the knees. Most tunics were made of wool or linen. (Job 30:18; Matthew 10:10; John 19:23) See also "linen."

Tychicus (TIK-ih-kus) is a name that means "fateful" or "important." He was a Christian from Asia. Paul gave him several important jobs to do. He stayed near Paul when Paul was in prison. (Acts 20:4; Ephesians 6:21-22; Colossians 4:7-9; 2 Timothy 4:12; Titus 3:12)

Tyre (TIRE) means "a rock." It was a large and important city in Phoenicia, which is now part of the country of Lebanon. The city was famous for its purple dye and glassware. Both Jesus and Paul visited Tyre. This city was destroyed by Alexander the Great. (Matthew 11:21; Mark 7:24-31; Acts 12:20; 21:3-7)

U

uncircumcised See "circumcision."

unclean is used to describe the state of a person, animal or action that was not pleasing to God. In the Old Testament God said certain animals were unclean. They were not to be eaten. If a person disobeyed this (or some other rule about being clean), that person was called unclean. He could not serve God until he was made clean again. (Genesis 7:2; Leviticus 11–15; Romans 14:14) See "clean."

unleavened bread (un-LEV-'nd bread) is bread made without yeast. This kind of bread is like a flat, thin cracker because it does not rise when it is baked. God told the Jews to use unleavened bread for the Passover Feast. (Exodus 12:20; Matthew 26:17-29; Mark 14:12-25)

Unleavened Bread, Day of, was the first day of the Feast of Unleavened Bread or Passover. (Luke 22:7)

upper room is an upstairs room in a house. Sometimes it was actually on the roof. This was often a room for guests. Jesus had his last supper with his followers in an upper room. (1 Kings 17:19; 2 Kings 1:2; Mark 14:14-15; Acts 1:12-13)

Ur was a great city thousands of years ago. Abraham lived there before God told him to move to Canaan. Ur was by the Euphrates River in the land that is today called Iraq. (Genesis 11:28-31)

Uriah (you-RY-uh) was a soldier in King David's army. His wife was Bathsheba. David wanted to marry Bathsheba; so he had Uriah killed in a battle. (2 Samuel 11) See also "Bathsheba."

Urim (YOUR-im) See "Thummim."

Uzzah (UZ-uh) touched the Holy Box when it was being brought to Jerusalem. God had said no one was to touch it. But Uzzah thought it was about to fall off the cart it was riding on. So, he put his hand on it to steady it. He died immediately. (2 Samuel 6:1-7; 1 Chronicles 13:1-14)

Uzziah (uh-ZY-uh) was a king of Judah. He was also called Azariah. He made the country stronger in many ways. At first he obeyed God and was successful. But when he became too proud, he did things he should not have done. He was given a skin disease as punishment. (2 Kings 15:1-3; 2 Chronicles 26:1-23; Isaiah 6:1)

V

Vashti (VASH-ty) was the wife of Ahasuerus, king of Persia. He had a banquet where many men were drunk. The king told Queen Vashti to come let the men see how beautiful she was. But she refused to do it and was removed as queen. This made it possible for Esther to become queen. (Esther 1:5-20)

veil (VALE) is a head covering usually worn by women. Sometimes the veil also covered the lower part of the face to hide the person's identity. Rebekah wore a veil in the Old Testament. This probably was to show that she was not married. (Genesis 24:65; Song of Solomon 4:1; Isaiah 3:19)

vest, holy, is often called the "ephod." This was a special type of clothing for the priests in the Old Testament. The holy vest for the high priest had gold and gems on it. The Urim and Thummim were attached to the holy vest. (Exodus 25; 28; 39) See also "High Priest" and "Thummim."

virgin (VUR-jin) is a woman or girl who has not had sexual relations. (Genesis 24:16; Deuteronomy 22:15-28; Isaiah 7:14; Matthew 1:23; Luke 1:34)

vision (VIZ-zhun) is like a dream. A vision could come to a person when he is awake or asleep. God used visions to tell people what he wanted them to do, to teach them something or to let them know something that was going to happen. (Genesis 15:1; Daniel 2:19; Acts 9:10-12; 10:3-19; 11:5; 16:9-10; 18:9)

vow is a special and serious promise. It is often made to God. (Acts 18:18; 21:23)

W

watchman was a guard. A watchman stood on top of the city walls watching for any danger. Watchmen also guarded crops in the field at harvest time. (2 Samuel 18:24-27; 2 Kings 9:17-20; Psalm 127:1)

way "The Way" was one of the earliest names given to Christians. Jesus said he was "the way" to reach God. So, Christians who follow Jesus' way are led to heaven and never-ending friendship with God. (John 14:6; Acts 9:2; 19:9,23; 24:14)

wedding is an event when a man and a woman become husband and wife. In Bible times a wedding was often celebrated for a week or more. Jesus did his first miracle at a wedding feast. He turned water into wine. (Matthew 22:1-14; Luke 14:8; John 2:1-11)

weights and measurements of Bible times. See "Weights and Measures" chart on page 125.

Western Sea See "Mediterranean Sea."

widow (WIH-doe) is a woman whose husband has died. Christians are told to take care of widows. One widow in the New Testament loved God so much that she gave all the money she had to him. (Luke 21:2-4; 1 Timothy 5:3-4; James 1:27)

winepress was a pit where grapes were mashed to get the juice out. People stepped on the grapes. The

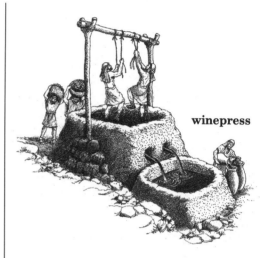

winepress

juice ran out into another container. The winepress is sometimes used to describe how God will punish people. When they sinned terribly, God would allow enemy armies to defeat them as if they were grapes crushed in a winepress. (Deuteronomy 15:14; Judges 6:11; Lamentations 1:15)

wisdom (WIZ-d'm) means understanding what is really important in life. This wisdom comes from God. The New Testament teaches that if you ask God for wisdom, he will give it to you. (1 Kings 4:29-30; Proverbs 1:2,7; Matthew 25:1-13; Acts 6:10; Colossians 3:16; James 1:5; 3:13-18)

wise men, or "magi," was a name for men who studied the stars. Some

TABLE OF WEIGHTS AND MEASURES

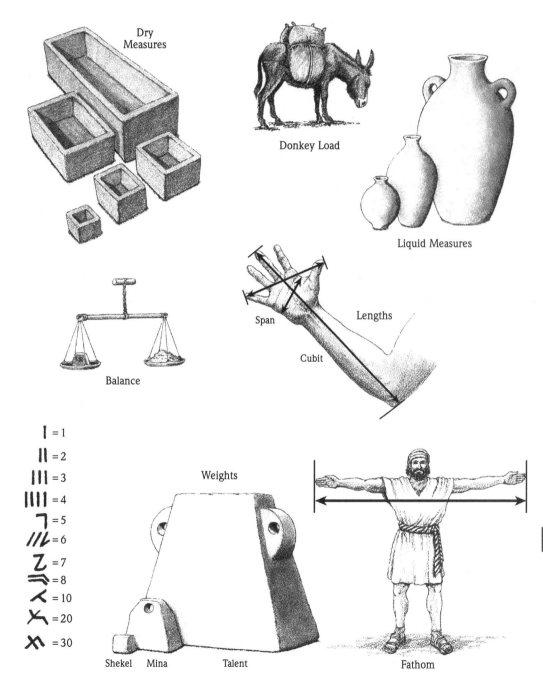

Dry Measures

Donkey Load

Liquid Measures

Balance

Span

Lengths

Cubit

| = 1
|| = 2
||| = 3
|||| = 4
⌐ = 5
//⌐ = 6
Z = 7
⤳ = 8
� = 10
⤸ = 20
𝕏 = 30

Weights

Shekel   Mina   Talent

Fathom

W

wise men followed a star from the East and brought gifts to Jesus when he was born. (Matthew 2:1-12)

witchcraft means using the power of the devil to do magic. (Deuteronomy 18:10; 2 Chronicles 33:6; Galatians 5:20)

witness (WIT-ness) is someone who tells what he has seen or what he knows. The apostles were witnesses for Christ because they told people that Jesus is the Son of God. (Acts 1:8,22; 2:32; 22:14-15)

woman, slave, is also called a concubine. She was a woman who may have been captured by a man during a war. Or he may have bought her as a slave. She was like a second-class wife whose main purpose was to have children for him. (Genesis 36: 12; 2 Chronicles 11:21)

word in the Bible often means God's message to us in the Scriptures. (1 Peter 1:24-25; 1 John 2:14) Jesus is called the "Word" because he shows us what God is like. (John 1:1-5,14)

world is used two different ways in the New Testament. It can mean the planet (Earth) where we live. It can also mean the people on this earth who follow Satan. Satan is called "the prince of this world." Christians are taught to love and obey God, instead of following the world's teaching of pleasing themselves. (Romans 12:2; Ephesians 2:2; 1 John 2:15-17; 5:4-5)

worship is to praise and serve God. When we worship God, we show that we accept him as the ruler of our lives. (Exodus 34:14; Matthew 28:9; Luke 4:8; John 4:20-24; James 1:27; Revelation 19:4-5)

X-Y

Xerxes (ZERK-sees) See "Ahasuerus."

yeast (YEEST) is an item used to make bread and cake rise. "Yeast" is sometimes used in the New Testament to stand for a person's influence over others. It can be either bad or good. (Mark 8:15; Luke 13:21) See also "unleavened bread."

yoke is a wooden frame that fits on the necks of animals to hold them together while working. Two oxen were often yoked together to pull

a farmer's plow. The word "yoke" is also used to mean the work a person is to do. (Deuteronomy 21:3; 2 Chronicles 10:4-11; Matthew 11:29)

Z

Zacchaeus (za-KEE-us) was a Jewish tax collector in the city of Jericho. He worked for the Romans, collecting taxes from his fellow Jews. He was a short man and once climbed a sycamore tree so he could see Jesus over the crowd of people. Jesus went home with Zacchaeus that day, and it changed Zacchaeus' life. (Luke 19:1-8)

Zadok (ZAY-dok) was a priest who helped King David several times. When David was dying, Zadok helped make sure Solomon became king in David's place. (2 Samuel 15:24-36; 17:15-21; 1 Kings 1:18-45; 2:35; 1 Chronicles 15:11-13)

Zarephath (ZAIR-eh-fath) was a Canaanite town where Elijah stayed with a widow. She let him stay in an upstairs room. Because she shared with Elijah, God made it possible for her to have plenty of food when she normally would have run out. (1 Kings 17:8-24; Luke 4:25-26)

Zealots (ZEL-ots) were a group of Jewish men who were also called "Enthusiasts." They hated the Romans for controlling their home country and planned to force them out. Simon, the apostle, had been a Zealot. (Luke 6:15; Acts 1:13)

Zebedee (ZEB-uh-dee) was a fisherman on Lake Galilee. He and his wife Salome had two sons, James and John, who became apostles. (Matthew 4:21-22; Mark 1:19-20)

Zechariah (ZEK-uh-RY-uh) was the name of 28 people in the Bible, including:

Zechariah, father of John the Baptist, was a Jewish priest in New Testament times. Read the interesting story about what happened to him when the angel told him he was going to be a father. (Luke 1:5-25,57-80)

Zechariah, king of Israel, ruled for only six months. He was murdered by Shallum. (2 Kings 14:29; 15:8-12)

Zechariah, son of Berekiah, was a prophet who wrote the next-to-the-last book in the Old Testament. He wrote about the rebuilding of Jerusalem. (Ezra 5:1; 6:14; Zechariah 1:1-7; 7:1-8)

Zechariah, son of Jehoiada, was a priest who taught people to serve God. But he was murdered in the Temple. (2 Chronicles 24:20-25; Matthew 23:35)

Zedekiah (ZED-eh-KY-uh) was the name of a king and two false prophets.

Zedekiah, son of Josiah and Hamutal, was the last king of Judah. He turned against the king of Babylon. This caused Jerusalem to be destroyed by Nebuchadnezzar. (2 Kings 24:16−25:7)

Zedekiah, son of Kenaanah, was a false prophet during the time of King Ahab. (1 Kings 22:1-24)

Zedekiah, son of Maaseiah, was a false prophet in Babylon during the time of Jeremiah. (Jeremiah 29:21-23)

Zephaniah (zef-uh-NY-uh) was a prophet who lived when Josiah was king of Judah. He wrote the short book of Zephaniah. It tells of God's punishment of both Judah and their enemies. But the book closes with hope that God's people will return from captivity.

Zerubbabel (zeh-RUB-uh-bull) was made governor of Jerusalem by Cyrus, king of Persia, after the Jews had been in captivity in Babylon for 70 years. He led the group of Jews who rebuilt the Temple. (Ezra 2:2; 3:2-11; 5:2)

Ziba (ZY-buh) was a servant of Saul. David put him in charge of looking after Saul's crippled son, Mephibosheth. Ziba was not always honest. (2 Samuel 9:1-11; 16:1-4; 19:24-30)

Zion (ZY-on) was a hill inside the city of Jerusalem. Later, the name Zion, or Sion, was used to mean all of Jerusalem. In the New Testament, Mount Zion is sometimes even used as a name for heaven. (Hebrews 12:22; Revelation 14:1)

Ziphites (ZIF-ites) were the people of the city of Ziph. It was about 25 miles south of Jerusalem. Twice David hid there while running from Saul. Both times the Ziphites told Saul that David was there. (1 Samuel 23:14-28; 26:1-25; Psalm 54)

Zipporah (zih-PO-ruh) was the wife of Moses. She was from the land of Midian. He met her there when he had to run away from Egypt. Moses made a good impression by helping her when some shepherds had caused her trouble. (Exodus 2:15-22; 18:1-7)

zither (ZITH-ur) was a type of musi-

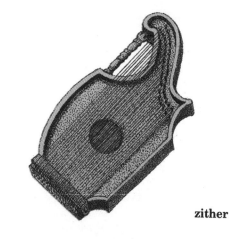

zither

cal instrument that had about 40 strings on it. (Daniel 3:5,7,10,15)